Race

The Biological and Social Meaning of Race

Edited by
RICHARD H. OSBORNE
University of Wisconsin
Madison, Wisconsin

W. H. Freeman and Company
San Francisco

301.0422
Os l b
122867
Sept. 1982

Library of Congress Catalog Card Number: 75-150652
ISBN: 0-7167-0934-1 (paper); 0-7167-0935-X (cloth)

Printed in the United States of America

123456789

Contents

Preface

There are probably few topics of greater moment than that of race. The subject touches the lives of us all, at all levels of education, and in all occupations. Everyone is aware that because of his ancestry, he is physically different from some people but quite similar to others. It is on the basis of this lay observation that most people apply the term *race*, ask questions concerning the practical meaning of race differences that they observe, construct their prejudices, and formulate the philosophies by which they order their own lives in respect to the race phenomenon.

The objective of this book is to discuss questions on race in a matter-of-fact and unemotional manner, presenting the most solid work of the scientific community and ignoring the brushfires around its edges. Recognized authorities in those academic areas relevant to race questions were asked to prepare the essays presented here in order to cover the topic from many different angles and disciplines. All of the essays, except "The Meaning of Race" by William W. Howells and the appendix, "The History and Nature of Race Classification" by Richard H. Osborne, were first published in the *Eugenics Quarterly*, now called *Social Biology*. The essays were then modified, with permission of the authors and that journal, for publication here in order to improve their suitability for students and lay readers.

The purpose of these essays is to present in a factual but nontechnical way the essential biological and social foundations of race and the consequences of these foundations. Each essay is preceded by a brief abstract by the editor, an abstract which is intended to organize the major points of the essay for the reader, as well as to prepare him mentally for and to direct his attention to the discussion within the article. By reading the preface, introduction, and abstracts in sequence, the reader can easily grasp the main messages of both the individual essays and the book as a whole.

Because prejudice and fear are usually based upon misunderstandings, which, in turn, are often the result of mere sematics, a glossary of the terms employed in the discussions of race has been included. The appendix gives a brief overview of the history and implications of race studies and racial classifications. The inclusion of references with each essay makes it possible for the reader to examine the literature and draw his own conclusions about various aspects of this increasingly important topic.

The articles originally published in *Eugenics Quarterly* from which essays in this volume were adapted are the following:

Baker, Paul T. 1966. Human biological variation as an adaptive response to the environment. *Eugen. Quart.* 13: 81-91.

Campbell, Arthur A. 1965. Fertility and family planning among nonwhite married couples in the United States. *Eugen. Quart.* 12: 124-131.

Damon, Albert. 1969. Race, ethnic group, and disease. *Soc. Biol.* 16: 69-80.

Dobzhansky, Theodosius. 1963. Genetics of race equality. *Eugen. Quart.* 10: 151-160.

Hulse, Frederick S. 1964. The paragon of animals. *Eugen. Quart.* 11: 1-10.

Hiernaux, Jean. 1968. Ethnic differences in growth and development. *Eugen. Quart.* 15: 12-21.

Kiser, Clyde V. 1968. Trends in fertility differentials by color and socio-economic status in the United States. *Eugen. Quart.* 15: 221-226.

Osborn, Frederick. 1963. Eugenics and the races of man. *Eugen. Quart.* 10: 103-109.

Pettigrew, Thomas F. 1964. Race, mental illness, and intelligence: A social psychological view. *Eugen. Quart.* 11: 189-215.

Purcell, Francis P., and Maurie Hillson. 1966. The disadvantaged child: A product of the culture of poverty, his education, and his life chances. *Eugen. Quart.* 13: 179-184.

RICHARD H. OSBORNE

April 1971

The Biological and Social Meaning of Race

Introduction

The Meaning of Race

WILLIAM W. HOWELLS
Department of Anthropology
Harvard University
Cambridge, Massachusetts

The concept of "race" continues to give so much trouble because it actually combines and compounds several separate problems, each one difficult enough in itself. It has been suggested, from time to time, that the word "race" be abolished, but it is unlikely that doing so would cause the numerous biological, social, and psychological facts relative to what is called "race" to go away.

Perhaps the least difficult problem is to define race in terms of its appropriate biological model, that is, the variation of populations within a typical animal *species*.[1] We might begin with a brief reference to one of the basic pillars of race and of *evolution* itself—Mendel's law of segregation. In simplest terms, this states that inheritance rests, not on blends of parental qualities, but on combinations of parental *genes*, units that preserve their own particular nature unchanged through the generations. Every individual is a new combination of existing genes. He is most like his parents because he draws his supply of genes from them; but he differs from them both, and from his brothers and sisters, because of the unique way the genes he has inherited have recombined. Thus, any community or population, even if it is small and inbred, is full of variety; and this variety cannot disappear, but rather continues to be expressed in new combinations of genes in each succeeding generation. Occasionally, new genes—usually mutated forms of older ones—appear as fresh material for variation. Certain genes and combinations are favored by a population's environment and thus become more common in that community or, in genetic terms, in the *gene pool* of that population. So, in turn, local populations come to differ in some aspects of their gene pools. This differentiation is the first step in evolution itself, although it is presented here in the simplest possible terms.

---

[1]Words defined in the Glossary (p. 173) are italicized the first time that they appear in each paper.

As are other animal species, the human species is composed of members capable of interbreeding. However, although biologically possible, breeding is not species-wide in actuality. Individuals are assorted into local populations, and mating usually occurs between individuals who are members of one population. Some interpopulation mating takes place, usually between members of adjacent populations.

These populations of a species are differentiated over time by the basic processes of evolution: to some degree by accidental changes in gene proportions; and, to a great degree, by natural *selection* and *adaptation* assigning different fates to existing gene combinations and to newly mutated genes (Mayr, 1963). Thus, the genetic structure and gene pools of different populations are distinct in *gene frequencies* and combinations and in the visible features of their members. If we were to create a simple model, we might show the difference between populations as proportional to the geographic distance between them, both because of gene exchange between nearer populations and because of different specific local adaptations to different environments.

This then is the picture of a widespread animal species. If its populations are strung out along one dimension, as along the coastline of a continent, these will differ by small steps, though not necessarily in a constant trend, so that more distant populations will differ most markedly. If the species is distributed very broadly in two dimensions, as toward the interior of the continent as well as along the coast, differentiation and adaptation of populations will be more complex. There will, however, be the same tendency for gradual change in gene frequencies, with greater differences occurring between populations at the geographical extremes. In actuality, terrain and climate do not vary so continuously as to lead to such a well-regulated progression of gradual change as we might hypothesize. At some points, barriers or environmental shifts may be expected to lead to great discontinuities between populations.

Zoologists collecting data on animal populations record visible differences between them—their *morphology*—as in size, wing length, or markings of birds, or in patterns of spotting on frogs and snails. For some populations, the genetic bases for morphological differences can be determined, as geneticist Theodosius Dobzhansky has done in his many studies of the fruit fly, *Drosophila*. In some cases, the relation to the environment via function or adaptation can be discerned; in others, it cannot, and the differences are recorded simply as a measure of biological "distance" between two populations (Howells, 1966).

Thus, considerable local and regional diversity among the populations of a species can be described. The species, of course, is the real and ultimate unit. Subdivisions of it, though also real, are arbitrary, and there is no natural or generally accepted criterion for establishing them.[2] Zoologists have generally used the term "subspecies" when a fairly clear discontinuity between populations can be shown. The most favored criterion for determining such discontinuity is that if 75% of group A can be distinguished in some feature from all of group B, the two are accepted as separate subspecies. This alone demonstrates the necessarily arbitrary nature of the classification. Beyond this, zoologists have, in the past, been driven to the use of various other terms for locally different population groups: races, varieties, etc. The establishment of subdivisions of a species is an arbitrary and slippery matter, although the population variety is real. In some cases, the subdivisions may be relatively so clear that assigning of subspecies is a matter zoologists can readily agree on; but this need not be so. As an example, the Old World monkeys present cases in which agreement is poor.

All of these concepts about species and subdivisions provide a framework into which man can be fitted readily. The only manipulation required is to take the human species at a time—unfortunately well in the past—when its distribution depended on travel by foot or the very simplest of water craft. We might select a point just at the end of the Pleistocene epoch, about ten thousand years ago, although we could choose one considerably further back. In simplified terms, we may visualize a Stone Age human species dispersed on all six continents in local populations with a degree of differentiation among them at least approximating what we know from more modern times. We do not have to ask here what were the sources of the differentiation— such as *genetic drift* or selection—since other writers in this volume will deal at length with these. We note only that this differentiation is what, more in man than in other animals, is called "race."

In most respects, the human situation fits the zoological model well. The most distant populations were in general the most unlike morphologically and were so recognizably distinct as to deserve subspecies rank by the usual criteria. However, the whole species could not then and can not now be divided into such "subspecies," because there was then and is today too much continuity and local variation.

Nevertheless, anthropologists have been bedeviled by the compulsion to classify for some two hundred years. The above exposition of the actual zoological nature of race should show why no two classifiers have arrived at the same result (though much general agreement is possible)

---

[2] See the Appendix (p. 161) for a brief discussion of racial classifications and the attempt to model them after zoological classifications for animal populations.

and why, in fact, formal classification is doomed to failure before it begins. This failure in the classifying mechanism has been used by some writers as a reason for rejecting the idea of race itself and the use of the term. Granted that there are limits on the precision with which either the concept or the term can be applied, nonetheless the variation in the populations remains.

Viewing human differentiation and distribution from another perspective, Livingstone (1962) has stated that there are no races; there are only *clines*. This means that, instead of being entities in themselves, races are simply statistical combinations of adaptive features which have geographical gradients—of skin color, for example, getting gradually darker as you go from north to south; of hair form getting less wooly as you go from Africa across India to northeast Asia; of faces becoming less flat and noses more pointed as you go from northeast Asia to Europe. There are also various trends that could be cited in non-visible characters, such as blood types. This concept of clines is much more sophisticated than the first kind of rejection of classifying techniques and is mainly a denial that races are distinct, discrete units, which is what I have been trying to say.

Another essential point that must be stressed is the great genetic variation *within* each population. It is not a function of the size or isolation of a population; some small communities in New Guinea appear to harbor greater variation in skin color than larger populations in Europe. The variation between neighboring populations consists only of a small displacement of the separate ranges of variation, which otherwise overlap to a great extent. In fact, for many traits, the variation may overlap widely between racial groups that could be called separate subspecies in terms of other traits. Variation of both kinds, within and between groups, is genetically the same and is an essential of evolution.

This then is the zoological and respectable view of race. It is ably amplified in other chapters. It is difficult to define, but many definitions by biologists and anthropologists at least get a hand-hold on it. To cite one I have offered elsewhere, races are the local limitations in the total variation in man, and race is not only a respectable but a most necessary object of study.

But what a change in the word "race" when we go from the scientific to the practical. We are in the twentieth century, not in the time when "populations" were wandering bands of hunters on foot. Contact between populations that differed little across the distance range that any one individual could cover has been replaced by contact between populations that differ in extremes. Africans from populations of the Slave Coast have been geographically juxtaposed to Europeans, mostly from the British Isles, in a North America to which both were strangers. But these two groups, like the Indian groups the first settlers found here, each came from widely separate parts of the original species range, in which long ago their respective *genotypes* had become in many respects sufficiently adapted and stabilized so that a few centuries in a different environment could not perceptibly modify them by the same processes of development that had been going on over time in their own populations. As long as they continued to mate with members of their own or similar populations from within the human species range, they continued to maintain by cultural barriers the population separateness formerly imposed by geographic barriers.

The confrontation of peoples from different parts of the species range has occurred as a result of migrations in various parts of the world, from Greenland to Australia. Certainly, in the United States, this confrontation has produced a different connotation of the word "race," distorting the more straightforward understanding of natural human variation I have outlined. The primary meaning of "race" has become Negro-white difference, not the facts of human history. The words "race riot" evoke only one understanding. And in trying to make a contribution from a scholarly and scientific point of view, the most difficult step to achieve has been to break down the hard assumptions that follow from the connotation of the word race produced by modern social confrontations. And the central and most recalcitrant assumption is that Negroes are on the average inferior to whites in mental capacity.

Either refuting or substantiating this assumption is impossible with present scientific knowledge and information. The evidence for the assumed inferiority is essentially that of I.Q. tests in which Negroes have consistently averaged lower scores than whites used for comparison, or have shown a range of scores of which only a small proportion surpasses the white mean score, all this over a long period of testing. The problems are those of an interpretation that adheres to scientific principles. Let us refer in part back to the earlier discussion of the nature of race.

First of all, intelligence is hardly a unitary character, even if forced into a single scale by I.Q. tests. Much work in human and animal psychology indicates that intelligence consists of differing faculties (see, e.g., Fuller and Scott, 1954) combined or substituted for one another in different ways for which the test situation may not provide an adequate measure. On the other hand, it has also been demonstrated that there is considerable individual genetic variation involved in these various faculties. Just as individuals cannot be asserted to be identical, neither can the gene pools of various populations. There is no reason why populations could not differ to some degree in the genes controlling intelligence and behavior. Therefore, it cannot be shown that *no* racial differences in intelligence exist.

One of the ways that the species has evolved, and an important reason it has been so successful, is the development of adaptability—the capacity of a population to respond effectively to different environments rather than to increase its difference from other populations by becoming strongly adapted to one particular environment alone. For example, while skin may be light or dark as a climatic adaptation, this does not importantly limit a population's adaptability to another climate.

Man's adaptability, or flexibility, his capacity to respond to the demands of his environment, is important when considering average differences between populations or races. This is particularly true for intelligence, which is behavioral and subject to even greater environmental modification than are physical traits. In determining whether or not there are racial differences in intelligence, both the effect of environment on development and imperfections in intelligence test data must be considered. The problems of intelligence testing have been dealt with often and fully elsewhere: the fact that tests cannot avoid measuring learning rather than innate capacity; the interference of negative attitudes toward testing and learning derived from home and parents; and so on. The point here is that there is little control over elements of the evidence—the test data and the environmental factors that modify intelligence and behavior—which means that the question of racial differences in intelligence cannot be answered scientifically. To scientists concerned with procedure, the uncontrolled factors still seem ample to overlap any genetic difference that might exist (see Commoner, 1963). In all honesty, therefore, scientists must decline to see the existence of racial variation in mental ability at this stage.

Let us consider another aspect of the race problem. This has to do with various strategies or suggested policies of different groups toward the phenomenon of race. One such strategy is the attempt of the great majority of anthropologists and allied scientists to inform the public of the nature of race and of the scientific conviction that this nature affords no foundation for concepts of racial inferiority or superiority. On several occasions, formal explanatory statements have been drawn up, the last under the auspices of UNESCO by a well-qualified panel which met at the International Congress of Anthropological and Ethnological Sciences in 1964 in Moscow. I think it is fair to say that my exposition on the nature of race is in accord with that statement. The great difficulty is that such statements, to be correct, must incorporate technical ideas and a sufficiently detailed exposition of the biology involved, and this is simply not easily assimilated by the general public. No effective way has been found, by such literary efforts, to stem the tendency of ordinary citizens to associate marked differences in ability or behavior with marked differences in skin color.

In addition, the physical anthropologists are in a peculiar situation. Because of their long-time interest in evolution, race, and physical variation, anthropologists are considered by the public to be equipped to make assessments of the behavioral and mental aspects of man—which they are not. It was the psychologists, in fact, who let the bull out of the pen with their development of devices for measuring and testing intelligence, and some leading psychologists, despite the fact they are not geneticists, continue to express a belief in genetic causes behind racial differences in intelligence scores. It is therefore not to be expected that anthropologists alone should go and catch the bull. Among anthropology, psychology, genetics, and sociology, it is difficult to see where the scientific responsibility lies.

Another policy is that of the racists, extreme or otherwise. Obviously, such writers use the same data on racial differences, but do not examine it for qualifications and deficiencies, interpreting what might be as what is. Their approach is that of the lawyer, who uses only those findings that support his case, not that of the scientist, who weighs all the evidence on its merit. In general, the racists' purpose is political action along racial lines.

A third policy—the other extreme from the racists—is generally, if inappropriately, called that of the egalitarians. It is the stance of some social anthropologists and sociologists. These writers say, or seem to say, that all races are indeed equal in endowment, instead of saying that the races cannot be shown to be unequal. Egalitarians are in fact so affronted by the idea of race as to deny its existence, or even to state that "there is no white race . . . there never was a white race . . . there is not now and never has been either a black race or a yellow race" (Fried, 1965). This may be good-hearted, but it is an impatient approach that probably does little to help such efforts at explanation as the 1964 UNESCO statement, a statement to which such writers give no sign of subscribing.

The race controversy has continued a long time with, strangely, little shift in positions or new data. Recently, scientists of standing—such as Ingle (1965) and Shockley (1967), a physiologist and a physicist respectively, and both members of the National Academy of Sciences—have suggested reopening the question of genetic differences in capacity, with new and more intensive investigations, perhaps even with massive governmental support. They feel that such research has been blocked by social liberal-mindedness in the pertinent sciences, this feeling being a more mild version of the belief of some racists that a communist conspiracy of suppression is at work. Now, it is probable that many geneticists, psychologists, and other scientists are reluctant to undertake such work, perhaps because of a distaste for the idea of inequality and its political effects, but more likely because present research tools are unsatisfactory. This kind of investigation is, therefore, not one that attracts the efforts of active research workers. It has been claimed that intimidation of students of race differences is a factor—and certainly such suggestions as those of Shockley and Ingle have met with strong opposition—but I doubt that this is the basic reason for any lag in research.

As genetic psychologists pointed out some time ago (Woodworth, 1941), heredity and environment are as inseparable for the realization of intellectual capacity as for anything else. As Frederick Osborn has said, (1940, and in "Races and the Future of Man" in this book) the more the environment is improved and equalized, the more important heredity becomes in differentiating individuals, and, therefore, groups. The only experiment that could settle the question of racial differences would be the elimination of all intervening factors by a general equalization of the environment, as suggested a generation ago. And this program, slow and difficult as it may be, is pretty clearly the only practical one.

REFERENCES

Commoner, B., et al. 1963. Science and the race problem. *Science* 142: 558–561.

Fried, M. H. 1965. A four-letter word that hurts. *Saturday Review*, October 2, 1965. Pp. 21–23, 35.

Fuller, J. S., and J. P. Scott. 1954. Genetic factors affecting intelligence. I. Heredity and learning ability in infrahuman mammals. *Eugen. Quart.* 1:28–43.

Howells, W. W. 1966. Population distances: Biological, linguistic, geographical, and environmental. *Curr. Anthrop.* 7: 531–540.

Ingle, D. J. 1965. Racial differences and the future. *Science* 147: 375–379.

Livingstone, F. B. 1962. On the non-existence of human races. *Curr Anthrop.* 3: 279–281.

Mayr, E. 1963. *Animal species and evolution.* Cambridge, Mass.: Harvard Univ. Press.

Osborn, F. 1940. *Preface to eugenics.* New York: Harper.

Shockley, W. 1967. A "try simplest cases" approach to the heredity-poverty-crime problem. *Proc. Natl. Acad. Sci.* 57: 1767–1774.

Woodworth, R. S. 1941. *Heredity and environment.* Bull. 47. New York: Social Sciences Research Council.

Biological Factors

Biological species are genetically closed systems; races are genetically open ones. Mankind has existed as a single species since at least the middle of the Pleistocene epoch, some half a million years ago. This unity has been maintained by the continuous, sometimes slow, but unfailing gene flow between neighboring clans, tribes, nations, and races. Furthermore, the genetic oneness of mankind has been growing steadily since the development of material culture has made travel between different parts of the world progressively easier and more rapid. Nonetheless, every human being is in some respects unlike any other. This diversity, whether of individuals or of groups such as races should not be confused with inequality. Equality is a sociological, not a biological, ideal. In actuality, man's diversity is a blessing, not a curse, since it permits the full exploitation of all his possible environments.

Race Equality

THEODOSIUS DOBZHANSKY
The Rockefeller University
New York, New York

The crucial fact of our age is that people almost everywhere now take the idea of human equality quite seriously. It is no longer accepted as nature's law that people with darker skins are destined to be servants and those with lighter ones, masters. Children of those at the bottom of the social ladder no longer are agreeable to being placed automatically in an inferior position. Everyone is entitled to equality. But what is equality? On the authority of the Declaration of Independence, it is a self-evident truth "that all men were created equal." Yet we hear that biology and genetics have demonstrated conclusively that men are unequal. Do biology and genetics really contradict what the Declaration of Independence holds to be self-evident? Or are the words "equal" and "unequal" being used in different senses? Just what have biology and genetics discovered that is relevant to the problem of equality or inequality?

Two geometric figures are said to be equal if they are identical in size and shape and coincide when superimposed on each other. Human equality, whether of persons or of groups, obviously means nothing of this sort. We generally have no difficulty distinguishing between persons whom we meet; the similarity of so-called identical twins strikes us as something unusual and remarkable. In fact, no two persons, not even identical twins, are ever truly identical. Every human being is in some respects unlike any other. This is not something that modern biology has recently found, but a matter of simple observation, so amply documented by the experience of everyone that its validity can hardly be questioned. Every person is indeed individual, unique, and unrepeatable. However, diversity and unlikeness, whether of individuals or of groups such as races, should not be confused with inequality. Nor should the affirmation of equality be taken to imply identity or uniformity.

Biology and genetics have some relevance to the question of human equality. They have ushered in a new understanding of the nature and causes of human diversity. This nature resides in the remarkable chemical substances, the *deoxyribonucleic acids* (DNA),[1] which are the principal constituents of the *genes* carried in the *chromosomes* of *cell nuclei*.

Genes are the discrete units on the chromosome each of which has its own unique action or effect by virtue of the structure of its particular DNA. It is the genes that are passed from parent to child through the sex cells, not the traits, which the action of the genes affects in cooperation with an individual's environment. An individual receives pairs of genes from his parents—one member of each pair being of maternal and the other of paternal origin.

When the individual's sex cells—egg cells or spermatozoa—are formed, each sex cell receives one or the other—either the maternal or the paternal member of every gene pair, but not a mixture of the two. However, a sex cell that receives a maternal copy of a gene A may receive either the maternal or the paternal copy of the gene B, of the gene C, etc. It is estimated that there are at least thousands or tens of thousands of genes carried in each human sex cell and the possible number of different combinations of genes that a single human could inherit is greater than the number of atoms in the universe and vastly greater than the number of sex cells produced. So it is pretty simple to see that not even brothers and sisters, children of the same parents, are at all likely to have all the same genes. No matter how many people may be born, despite any possible "population explosion," a tremendous part of the potentially possible human nature will never be realized. A carping critic may remark that we hardly needed to learn genetics to discover what we know from everyday observations, i.e., that no two persons are ever alike. Genetics, does, however, demonstrate something less commonplace when applied to analysis of the racial diversity among men.

---

[1] Words defined in the Glossary (p. 173) are italicized the first time they appear in each paper.

We are inclined to treat the diversity of groups in a manner rather different from diversity of individuals. If asked to describe your brother, or a cousin, or a fellow next door, you will probably say that he is somewhat taller (or shorter), darker (or lighter), heavier (or slimmer) than you, and you may add that he is inclined to be kind or easily angered, lazy or impatient, etc. A person whose ancestors lived in America before Columbus is, however, likely to be referred to as an Indian, and one whose ancestors came from tropical Africa, as a Negro.

Up to a point, this is, of course, legitimate. People of African ancestry usually have such conspicuous traits as a dark skin, kinky hair, broad nose, full lips, etc. One should not, however, forget that individual Indians, or Negroes, differ among themselves as much as do persons of the white race or any other race or group. When a group of people is given a name, a stereotype is likely to be invented; and, oddly enough, the fewer persons of a given group one knows, the more rigid the stereotypes of what all Indians, or Negroes, or Irishmen, or Jews are supposed to be. Most unreasonable of all, persons are then likely to be treated not according to what they are as individuals, but according to the stereotype of the group to which they belong. This is as unwarrantable biologically as it ethically iniquitous.

Biologists have classified between a million and two million *species* of animals and plants. An individual animal belongs to a certain species. It is, for example, either a horse *(Equus caballus)* or an ass *(Equus asinus)* or a sterile species hybrid (mule); but it cannot belong to two species at the same time. Biologists are sometimes in doubt as to whether certain forms should be regarded as belonging to the same or to two different species; however, with enough material, and given careful study, the doubts can usually be resolved. There is, however, no agreement among anthropologists concerning how many races there are in the human species. When anthropologists and biologists started to describe and classify races of men and species of animals, they treated races the same way they treated species. Each was catalogued and given a name. But then difficulties arose. Opinions as to the number of races vary from three to more than two hundred. This is not a matter of insufficient data; the more studies are made on human populations, the less clear-cut the races become.

The difficulty is fundamental. Biological species are genetically closed systems; races are genetically open ones. Species do not interbreed and do not exchange *genes*, or do so rarely; they are reproductively isolated. The gene pools of the species man, chimpanzee, gorilla, and orang are quite separate; gene interchanges do not occur between these species. The biological meaning of this separation is evolutionary independence.

Two species may have arisen from a common ancestor who lived long ago, but they embarked on separate evolutionary courses when they became species. No matter how favorable a new gene arising by mutation in the human species may be, it will not benefit the species chimpanzee nor vice versa.

Not so with races. Mankind, the human species, has been a single evolutionary unit, at least since the mid-Pleistocene epoch (Ice Age). It continues to be a single unit, all segregations and apartheids notwithstanding. Wherever different human populations are sympatric, i.e., geographically intermingled in a common territory as castes or as religious or linguistic groups, some interbreeding and gene exchange takes place. More important still is the interbreeding and gene flow among populations of neighboring territories. It is a relative innovation in mankind that some racially distinct populations live sympatrically, like Negroes and whites over a considerable part of the United States. Before, say, 2000 B.C., the human races, like races of most animal species, were largely allopatric, i.e., living in different territories. However, the peripheral gene flow—the gene exchange between allopatric but neighboring populations, whether human or animal—is and always was a regular occurrence.

This continuous, sometimes slow, but unfailing gene flow between neighboring clans, tribes, nations, and races upholds the biological and evolutionary unity of mankind. There may be no recorded case of a marriage of an Eskimo with, say, a Melanesian or a Bushman, but there are genetic links between all these populations via the geographically intervening groups. In contrast with distinct species, a beneficial change arising in any population anywhere in the world may become a part of the common biological endowment of all races of mankind. This genetic oneness of mankind has been growing steadily since the development of material culture has made travel and communication between the inhabitants of different countries progressively more rapid and easier. What should be stressed, however, is that mankind has not become a meaningful biological entity just recently, since men began to travel often and far. The human species was such an entity even before it became recognizably human.

Races, on the contrary, are not, and never were, groups clearly defined biologically. The gene flow between human populations makes race boundaries always more or less blurred. Consider three groups of people, for example: Scandinavians, Japanese, and Congolese. Each individual in these groups will probably be easily placeable in one of three races —Caucasoid, Mongoloid, and Negroid. It will, however, be far from easy to delimit these races if one observes also the inhabitants of the countries geographically intermediate between Scandinavia, Japan, and the Congo, respectively. Intermediate countries have intermediate populations, or populations that differ in some characteristics from all previously outlined races. One may try to get out of the difficulty by recognizing several intermediate races; or else, one may speculate that the races were nicely distinct at some time in the past, and got mixed up lately owing to interbreeding. This helps not at all. The more races one sets up, the fuzzier their boundaries become. And the difficulty is by no means confined to man; it occurs as well in many biological species in which it cannot be blamed on recent interbreeding.

Populations that inhabit different countries differ more often in relative frequencies of genetically simple traits rather than in having any single trait present in all individuals of one population and always absent in another population. Not only are the differences thus relative rather than absolute, but, to make things still more complex, the variations of different characters are often independent or at least not strongly correlated. Some populations may be clearly different in a gene A but rather similar in a gene B, while other populations may be different in B but less so in A. This makes the drawing of any lines separating different races a rather arbitrary procedure and results in the notorious inability of anthropologists to agree on any race classification yet proposed. Race classifiers might have indeed preferred to find simple and tidy races, in which every person would show just the characteristics that his race is supposed to possess. Nature has not been obliging enough to make the races conform to this prescription. Exactly the same difficulties that a student of races encounters in classifying the human species are met with also by zoologists who work with animal species.

Much-needed light on the nature of population or race differences, whichever one chooses to call them, came from studies on the genetics of chemical constituents of the human blood. As far back as 1900, Landsteiner discovered four blood types, or blood groups, distinguishable by simple laboratory tests. These blood groups—called O, A, B, and AB—are inherited very simply, according to Mendel's laws. Brothers and sisters and parents and children may, and quite often do, differ in blood types. An enormous number of investigations have been made, especially in recent years, on the distribution of the blood types among peoples in various parts of the world. Any race or population can be described in terms of the percentages of the four blood types. Persons of all four types are found almost everywhere, but in different proportions. Thus, types B and AB are commonest among peoples of central Asia and India, type A in peoples of western Europe and in some American Indians, and many American Indian tribes have predominantly or even exclusively type O.

Several other blood group systems have been discovered, including the

Rhesus system, usually referred to as the Rh factor. The genes for these blood groups behave in general like those for the "classical" O-A-B-AB blood types. For example, one of the variants (*alleles*) of the Rhesus gene occurs much more often in the populations of Africa than elsewhere. But—mark this well—this gene does occur, albeit infrequently, in human populations almost everywhere in the world, and it is quite certain that it has not spread so widely owing to a Negro admixture in recent centuries.

These facts are profoundly significant. Consider the following situation, which is by no means unusual. A person of European origin, say an Englishman or a Frenchman, has O blood; his brother has B blood. In this particular respect, these brothers differ from each other; one of them resembles many American Indians who have O blood, and the other matches numerous persons in Asia and elsewhere who have B blood. Or else, one of the brothers may have the kind of Rhesus blood type most characteristic of the Africans, and the other brother may have blood more like a majority of his European neighbors. Such characteristics, of which the persons concerned are usually quite unaware, may become vitally important in some circumstances. If an individual with type O blood needs a blood transfusion, then blood from a donor of no matter what race will be safe, while the blood of the recipient's brother may be dangerous if that brother has A, B, or AB blood.

Though not different in principle from the genetics of blood types, the genetics of skin color and similar traits is considerably more complex. The color difference between Negro and white skin is due to joint action of several genes, each of which by itself makes the skin only a little darker or lighter. Geneticists have studied the inheritance of skin pigmentation for half a century; yet exactly how many genes are involved is still unknown. Skin color is obviously variable among the so-called "white" as well as among the "black" peoples, some individuals being darker and others lighter. If we were able to map the geographic distribution of each separate skin color gene as thoroughly as has been done for some blood group genes, the race differences would probably be resolved into gene frequency differences. It is fair to say that the studies on blood types and similar traits have, so far at least, helped more to explain the nature of races than to classify them.

Thus, every race includes persons with diverse genetic endowments. Genetic studies show that race differences are compounded of the same kinds of genetic elements in which individuals within a race also differ. An individual must always be judged according to what he is, not according to the place of origin of his ancestors. Races may be defined as populations which differ in frequencies, or in prevalence, of some genes. Race differences are relative, not absolute.

This modern race concept, based on findings of genetics, appears to differ from the traditional view so much that it has provoked some misunderstanding and opposition. The use of traits such as blood groups to elucidate the nature of the races of which mankind is composed may seem a questionable procedure. To distinguish races, should one use, rather, traits like skin pigmentation in place of blood types? Some blood types can be found almost anywhere in the world; on the other hand, pale skins (other than albino) do not occur among the natives of equatorial Africa or of New Guinea, and black skins are not found among the natives of Europe. This objection is beside the point. The blood types are useful because their genetic nature is relatively simple and well understood. The classification of the human races need not be based on any one trait; the behavior of the blood types helps, however, to understand the behavior of other traits, including skin color.

To sum up, the races of man are not integrated biological entities of the sort that biological species are. Race boundaries are blurred by the more or less slow but long-sustained gene exchange. The number of races that should be recognized is arbitrary in the sense that it is a matter of convention and convenience whether one should give names to only a few "major" or also to a larger number of "minor" races. An anthropologist who maintains that there are exactly five or any other fixed number of races or who resolves to cut the Gordian Knot (mankind has no races) is nurturing illusions. On the other hand, there need be nothing arbitrary about race differences; human populations are racially distinct if they differ in the frequencies of some genes, and not distinct if they do not so differ. The presence of race differences can be ascertained, and if they are present, their magnitude can be measured.

The problem that inevitably arises in any discussion of individual and race equality is how consequential the differences among humans really are. Man's bodily structures do not differentiate him very strikingly from other living creatures; it is the psychic, intellectual, or spiritual side of human nature that is truly distinctive of man. Physical race differences supply only the externally visible marks by which the geographic origin of people, or rather of their ancestors, can be identified. The blood types, nose shapes, and skin colors of people whom we meet are much less important to us than their dispositions, intelligence, and rectitude.

The diversity of personalities would seem to be as great, and surely more telling, than the diversity of skin colors or other physical traits. And, though the biological basis of both kinds of diversity is the same in principle, it is different enough in its outward manifestations that the difference constitutes a genuine problem. This is the perennial *nature-nurture problem*. The confusion and polemics with which it was beset for a long time were due in part to the problem having been wrongly stated—which human traits are due to heredity and which to environment. No trait can arise unless the heredity of the organism makes it possible, and no heredity operates outside of environment. A meaningful way to state it is to ask what part of the diversity observed in a given population is conditioned by the genetic differences between persons composing this population, and what part is due to their upbringing, education, and other environmental variables. Furthermore, the issue must be investigated and solved separately for each function, trait, or characteristic that comes under consideration. Suppose one collects good data on the genetic and environmental components of the observed diversity in the intelligence quotients, or of the resistance to tuberculosis. This would not tell us anything about the diversity of temperaments or about resistance to cancer.

Even correctly stated, the nature-nurture problem remains a formidable one. Dogmatic statements abound on both the hereditarian and the environmentalist sides of the controversy, and most of them say much about their authors but not much about the subject at issue. The plain truth is that it is not known just how influential are the genetic variables in psychic or personality traits or how plastic these traits might be in different environments that can be contrived by modern technology, medicine, and educational methods. There is no way in practice to arrange for a large group of people to be brought up under controlled and uniform conditions in order to see how similarly or differently they would develop. The converse experiment—observing identical twins, individuals with similar heredities brought up in different environments —is possible, but opportunities for such observations are scarce.

Some partisans of human equality got themselves in the untenable position of arguing that mankind is genetically uniform with respect to intelligence, ability, and other psychic traits. Actually it is, I think, fair to say that whenever any variable trait in man has been at all adequately studied genetically, evidence has been found of at least some, though perhaps slight, contribution of genetic differences. Being equal has to be compatible with being different, and different in characters that are relevant to the specifically human estate, not alone in "skin-deep" traits like skin color.

The current civil rights movement in the United States has elicited a rash of racist pamphlets that pretend to prove, very "scientifically" of course, that races cannot be equal because they differ in the average brain size, the average I.Q., etc. Now, there is no reason to believe that small differences in the brain volumes are any indication of different mental capacities; the I.Q. tests are not reliable when administered to people of different sociocultural backgrounds, and in any case they cannot be taken as anything approaching a measurement of human worth. Be all that as it may, the striking fact—which not even the racists can conceal—is that the race differences in the averages are much smaller than the variations within any race. In other words, large brains and high I.Q.'s of persons of every race are much larger and higher than the averages for their own or any other race. And conversely, the low variants in every race are much below the average for any race. This is a situation quite analogous to what is known about race differences in such traits as blood groups and is in perfect accord with theoretical expectations in populations that exchange genes.

It is impossible in an article such as this one to summarize and to evaluate critically the abundant but often unreliable and contradictory data on the nature-nurture question regarding man. It is more useful to consider here some fundamentals that must be kept in mind in dealing with such data. An all too often forgotten and yet most basic fact is that the genes do not determine traits or characters, but rather the ways in which the organism responds to the environment. One inherits not the skin color and intelligence, but only genes which make the *development* of certain colors and intelligence possible. To state the same thing with a slightly different emphasis, the gene complement determines the path that the development of a person will take, given the sequence of the environments that this person encounters in the process of living. Any developmental process, whether physiological or psychological, can be influenced or modified by genetic as well as by environmental variables. The realization of heredity is manageable, within limits, by physiological and social engineering. What the limits are depends upon our understanding of the developmental processes involved. Modern medicine is able to control the manifestations of some hereditary diseases, which not so long ago were incurable. This does not make hereditary defects and diseases harmless or unimportant; even if they can be cured, it is better for the individual and for his society to have no necessity of being cured.

Although the mode of inheritance of physical and psychic traits in man is fundamentally the same, their developmental plasticity—the ability to respond to modifying influences of the environment—is different. There is no known way to alter the blood group with which a person is born; it is possible to modify one's skin color, making it somewhat darker or lighter by sun tanning or by lack of exposure to the sun; the development of personality traits is very much dependent on the family and social environments in which an individual is brought up and lives. The great *lability* of psychic traits is at least one of the reasons why it is so hard not only to measure precisely the role played by heredity in their variations, but even to prove unambiguously that some of these traits are influenced by heredity at all. The more environmentally labile a trait is, the more critical it is for its investigation to have the environment under control; this is difficult or impossible to achieve with man.

The great environmental plasticity of psychic traits in man is no biological accident. It is an important, even crucial, evolutionary adaptation that distinguishes man from other creatures, including those nearest to him in the zoological system. It is by brain, not by brawn, that man controls his environment. Mankind's singular and singularly powerful adaptive instrument is culture. Culture is not inherited through genes; it is acquired by learning from other human beings. The ability to learn, and thus to acquire a culture and to become a member of a society, is, however, given by the genetic endowment that is mankind's distinctive biological attribute. In a sense, human genes have surrendered their primacy in human evolution to an entirely new, nonbiological or superorganic agent—culture. However, it should not be forgotten that this agent is entirely dependent on the human genotype.

A pseudobiological fallacy—dangerous, because it is superficially so plausible—alleges that the differences in psychic traits among human individuals and races are genetically fixed to about the same extent as they are among races or breeds of domestic animals. This overlooks the fact that the behavior of a breed of horses or of dogs is always a part of a complex of characters that are deliberately selected by the breeders to fit the animal for its intended use. A hunting dog with a temperament of a Pekingese, a great Dane behaving like a fox terrier, a draft horse as high-strung as a race horse or vice versa—all these monstrosities would be worthless or even dangerous to their human masters. Man has seen to it that the genes that stabilize the desirable behavior traits in his domestic animals be fixed and the genes that predispose for variable or undesirable behavior be eliminated.

What is biologically as well as sociologically requisite in man is the exact opposite—not to fix rigidly his qualities; he must be able to learn whatever mode of behavior fits a job to be done, the mores of the group of which he happens to be a member, a conduct befitting the circumstances and opportunities. Man's paramount adaptive trait is his educability. The biological evolution of mankind has accordingly so shaped the human genotype that educability is a universal property of all nonpathological individuals. It is a diagnostic character of mankind as a species, not of only some of its races. This universality is no accident either. In all cultures, primitive or advanced, the vital ability is to be able to learn whatever is necessary to become a competent member of some group or society. In advanced civilizations, the variety of function has grown so enormously that learning has come to occupy a considerable fraction of the life span. Even where, as in India, a society was splintered for centuries into castes specialized for different occupations, the ability to learn new professions or trades has been preserved.

Champions of human equality have traditionally been environmentalists, conspicuously distrustful of genetic determinisms. Historically their attitude has been useful in counterbalancing the influence of those racist hereditarians who tried to justify the denial of equality of opportunity to most people on the pretext that the latter were genetically inferior. The environmentalists, however, went too far in their protest. They simply failed to understand that to be equal is not the same thing as to be alike. Equality is a sociological, not a biological, ideal. A society may grant equality to its citizens, but it cannot make them alike. What is more, in a society composed of genetically identical individuals, equality would be meaningless; individuals would have to be assigned for different occupations by drawing lots or in some other arbitrary manner. The ideal of equality of opportunity is precious, because it holds out a hope that persons and groups diverse in their endowments may enjoy a feeling of belonging and of partnership and may work for the common good in whatever capacity without loss of their human dignity. Men must be dealt with primarily on the basis of their humanity and also on the basis of their potentialities and accomplishments as individuals; the practice of treating them according to their race or color is a nefarious one.

Genetic diversity is a blessing, not a curse. Any society, particularly any civilized society, has a multitude of diverse vocations and callings to be filled, and new ones are constantly emerging. The human genetically secured educability enables most individuals of all races to be trained for most occupations. This is certainly the basic and fundamental adaptive quality of all mankind; yet this is in no way incompatible with a genetically conditioned diversity of preferences and special abilities. Music is an obnoxious noise to some, ecstatic pleasure to others. Some have a bodily frame that can be trained for championship in wrestling, or running, or sprinting, or weight lifting. Some can develop phenomenal abilities for chess playing, or painting, or composing poetry. Can anybody develop a skill in any of these occupations if he makes sufficient effort? Possibly many people could, to some extent. The point is, however, that what comes easily to some requires great exertion from others, and even then the accomplishment is mediocre at best. The willingness to strive derives, however, at least in part, from a feeling that the labor is rewarded by the thrill of accomplishment or in some other way. There is little stimulus to exert oneself if the results of the exertions are likely to be pitifully small. And it is also possible that there is such a thing as predisposition to striving and effort.

It is a perversion of the ethic of equality to endeavor to reduce everybody to a uniform level of achievement. "From each according to his ability" is the famous motto of Marxian socialism, and it behooves democracy to grant no less recognition to the diversity of human individualities. This is not an apology for "rugged individualism"; the "ruggedness" amounts often to indifference or even contempt for individualities of others. Equality is, however, not an end in itself, but a means to an end, which can only be the self-actualization of human individuals and the fullest possible realization of their socially valuable capacities and potentialities. Individuals and groups will arrange their lives differently, in accordance with their diverse notions of what form of happiness they wish to pursue. Their contributions to mankind's store of achievements will be different in kind and in magnitude. The point is that everyone should be able to contribute to the limit of his ability. To deny the equality of opportunity to persons or groups is evil, because it results in wastage of talent, ability, and aptitude, besides being contrary to the basic ethic of humanity.

RECOMMENDED READING

Carrington, R. 1963. *A million years of man.* Cleveland and New York: World Publishing Co.

Carson, H. L. 1963. *Heredity and human life.* New York: Columbia Univ. Press.

Dobzhansky, T. 1955. *Evolution, genetics and man.* New York: John Wiley. (Paperback, 1963.)

Dobzhansky, T. 1956. *The biological basis of human freedom.* New York: Columbia Univ. Press. (Paperback, 1960.)

Dobzhansky. T. 1962. *Mankind evolving.* New Haven: Yale Univ. Press.

Gardner, J. W. 1961. *Excellence.* New York: Harper.

Garn, S. M. 1961. *Human races.* Springfield, Ill.: Charles C. Thomas.

Grant, V. 1963. *The origin of adaptations.* New York: Columbia Univ. Press.

Hulse, F. S. 1963. *The human species.* New York: Random House.

Mayr, E. 1963. *Animal species and evolution.* Cambridge: Harvard Univ. Press.

Simpson, G. G. 1949. *The meaning of evolution.* New Haven: Yale Univ. Press. (Paperback, 1961.)

Simpson, G. G. 1961. *Principles of animal taxonomy.* New York: Columbia Univ. Press.

A successful animal species, one that has been capable of surviving through time, is adapted to its environment. Man's environment is cultural as well as physical, and he therefore has "more environments" to which he is adapted than any other animal. One important factor in man's ability to adapt to so many environments is his phenotypic plasticity—the capacity to change his physiological and behavioral responses to wide ranges of environmental fluctuation. Although this ability is an inherited characteristic of the species and as such may vary in some respects from population to population, racial differences in psychological accommodation and in physiological or developmental acclimatization may be due to stress experience as well as to genetic differences. At present, only the simplest adaptive responses with the fewest links have been traced to specific genetic or environmental influences.

Human Biological Diversity as an Adaptive Response to the Environment

PAUL T. BAKER
Department of Sociology and Anthropology
The Pennsylvania State University
University Park, Pennsylvania

Man, like any other animal *species*[1] that still survives, is adapted to his environment. This statement signifies only that at this point in time man is a successful animal on this planet with no immediate prospects of extinction. Of course it implies much more, since the physical and biological environments within which man exists are far broader than those of any other animal; and if we include as part of man's environment that distillate of human behavior called culture, then the breadth of man's *adaptation* is truly extraordinary.

When we inquire into the sources of the great adaptability of our

---

[1]Words defined in the Glossary (p. 173) are italicized the first time they appear in each paper.

species, two concepts are generally mentioned—race and culture. Both of these concepts are so broad and imprecise in meaning that they are poor scientific tools for the study of adaptation.

Culture can be a useful abstraction when used to categorize nonbiologically transmitted human information; but it can never completely explain any unit of human behavior, because man is a biological organism whose behavior is being explained. Thus, the accumulated information on how to sew an Eskimo parka is a product of Eskimo culture; but the adaptive value of the parka in permitting man to live in arctic cold also involves the motor skill of the maker and the physiological responses of the wearer.

Race is an equally unsatisfactory conceptual tool. It has limited research use and is often badly abused when the results of a study on one small segment of a race are extended to the whole group without a valid basis. To illustrate both the valid use and abuse of race as a research tool for studying human variation and adaptation, cases from environmental physiology may be cited. It has been shown that the skin of an American Negro absorbs more solar radiation than does white skin (Baker, 1958) because of its higher *melanin* content. Since in most classification systems "Negro" always means a high skin melanin, we may generalize that all Negroes in a nude condition will absorb more heat from the sun than whites. On the other hand, to cite a possible abuse, several investigators have found that the fingers of American Negro soldiers are "colder" in ice water than those of American white soldiers (Adams and Covino, 1958; Iampietro et al., 1959). While this difference appears to be the result of lower warm blood circulation in the Negro hands, the causes of this circulatory difference are unknown and may be unrelated to the traits associated with race. Thus, it would be pure speculation to generalize that most classificatory "Negroes" have colder fingers in ice water, particularly when we do not even know if Negro females test lower than white females.

We must use concepts far more specific than race and culture if we hope to understand how man has adapted to his varied environments and what role his biological variability has played in this adaptation.

SOURCES OF MAN'S ADAPTATION
TO THE ENVIRONMENT

Man owes his adaptive structure to the evolutionary process, which has provided him with a wide variety of adaptive mechanisms. Human populations may adapt to a new form of environmental stress by a mutational change being acted upon by *selection* with subsequent changes in *gene frequency* in the group subjected to the stress. Indeed, as recent studies have shown, this type of genetic adaptation of a population has probably been more common than had been assumed. However, the enormous range of adaptive mechanisms available to man are primarily the consequence of his increasing somatic and behavioral plasticity.

One of the trends in the evolution of mammals was the rise in adaptive phenotypic plasticity that increasingly allowed animals to vary their pattern of functioning and behavior in response to the information provided by the environment in which they developed. The most apparent aspect of increasing plasticity in man was the increasing ability to learn, and the most important single attribute for the development of culture is man's enormous learning capacity. In biological terms, this capacity might simply be conceived of as his great ability to pattern his behavior in response to environmental challenges.

Of equal consequence for adaptation to diverse environments is man's functional and morphological adaptive plasticity. This kind of plasticity is probably most familiar to us in its short-term manifestations. For example, temperature and altitude acclimatization are well-documented examples of modifications in the functioning of man that increase his performance capability in the face of new environmental stress. Other examples are the increase in muscle fiber size that accompanies exercise and the psychological process of accustomization that allows the organism to ignore distracting stimuli in the environment. Less well studied are the long-term adaptive changes that occur in human beings when they develop under particular types of environmental stress. For example, children who must exist in a calorie-deficient environment can do so for prolonged periods of time by cessation of growth which will later be made up (McCance and Widdowson, 1951) if the deprivation period is not of excessive length. In the same vein, man has the capacity to store excess calories in the form of fat so that they can later be used during periods of short calorie supply. Other examples include the increased size of the lungs and the heart that occurs in individuals who grow up in a high-altitude environment with its low oxygen pressure (Monge, 1948).

Thus, if we look closely at the problem of studying human adaptability, we see that man has such a large variety of environmental stresses to which he adapts and such a large variety of mechanisms available to him for adaptation that we are probably dealing with a unique set of interactions in each human population. In studying human variation, we must take great care to identify properly the stresses to which a given population has been exposed and to consider all of the means of adaptation man has available to solve the problem of survival in that particular environment.

Given the uniqueness of each adaptive pattern, we may still believe that the limitations of the human germ plasm are such that similar partial solutions to adaptive needs will be found in many populations. That this is indeed the case for cultural adaptation seems to be demonstrated by the independent inventions of such material culture items as house forms and agriculture. Biologically, the instances are even more impressive, since the existence of morphological and genetic traits that are clustered enough to permit racial classification indicates a common genetic response to selection.

In the remainder of this paper we will examine the role of man's biological variation in his adaptive structure and present some of the knowledge thus far available on man's adaptive biological responses to environmental stresses. The sources of man's biological adaptation may be arbitrarily categorized into four interrelated types: genetic adaptation, psychological accommodation, physiological acclimatization, and developmental acclimatization. The functional difference between genetic and the other three types of adaptation is apparent, since the latter all are part of adaptive plasticity. Let us first examine adaptation.

GENETIC ADAPTATION

The relationship between the variety of genetic structures of human populations and adaptation may be viewed from two perspectives: (1) the theoretical relationship established by genetic evolutionary theories, and (2) the demonstrable evidence that specific genetic variation had adaptive value. Studies of the way human genetic variability relates to human adaptation are largely the product of the past twenty years. Until the end of the 1940s most anthropologists were concerned with the search for nonadaptive inherited traits, which differed in various races, in the hope that prehistoric migration and population admixture could be reconstructed, much as the archaeologist reconstructs culture history from pottery designs.

Since this era the geneticist has forcefully pointed out that the body of evolutionary theory derived from genetic studies on other animals does not permit us to ignore adaptation in the interpretation of human variation. As will be seen, the well-established relationships remain few, and if the accumulated genetic theories were less conclusive, a majority of human biologists might still hold the view that most genetic variation in man is and was without adaptive significance. Let us, therefore, examine first the nature and strength of this theoretical structure.

Evolutionary Theory

At the base of the genetic explanation of evolution lies the simple mathematical principle generally referred to as the *Hardy-Weinberg law*, which points out that the gene randomization process that occurs in bisexually reproducing higher animals will not in itself change the frequency of genes in a population. But, as Sewall Wright (1943) showed mathematically, the size of a population and the frequency of a specific gene within it can influence a gene's chance of survival; this is known as *genetic drift*. In very small populations pure chance can lead to the loss of a gene with a fairly low frequency, while a gene with a very high frequency may completely replace its less frequent allele. This is a purely statistical concept, and the probability of these occurrences is strictly determined by population numbers and gene frequencies. The other ways the gene frequencies in a population may be modified are by (1) *mutation* and *chromosomal aberrations*, (2) gene flow in or out of the population, and (3) *selection* (any nonchance phenomena that leads to the greater or lesser reproduction of individuals possessing a given gene).

By themselves, mutational and chromosomal abberations cannot explain the major part of genetic variation among human populations, since they are similar in kind and frequency for all groups; without selection or *drift* to fix these variants, no population variation would develop. Gene flow is meaningless to our basic problem since we are asking how differentiation in genetic structure initially occurred within our species, which is, by definition, a breeding unit.

Thus, only two explanations for genetic variation remain—the Sewell Wright genetic drift explanation and the process of selection. Drift first presented an attractive explanation since man in his hunting and gathering days lived in very small bands thinly spread over large areas. If we assume that he was then endogamous, mating within his own band, there existed a perfect situation for drift effects, with those genes lost or becoming more frequent differing between bands. Undoubtedly, drift did have some effect. It has been demonstrated, fairly conclusively, to be the cause of some of the variation in other animal species, and at least one example has been presented with strong evidence for man (Giles, 1965). However, drift is a very unsatisfactory explanation for the major variations in the human population *genotypes*. For one thing, if early man had been completely endogamous, he would have rapidly developed into several different species as did other endogamous animal populations. More important, the genetic drift theory is a probability theory; so that while the probability of two populations developing a difference in the frequency in one gene due to drift is fairly high, the probability of their developing multiple gene differences is progressively lower. Indeed, it is statistically improbable that two populations could have developed a high frequency difference in even one hundred genes over the period of time that our species existed as hunters and gatherers. Since we know that even the few major *morphological* characteristics on which broad racial classifications are based seem to relate to a large number of genotype differences, we must conclude that drift is an unsatisfactory explanation for most of the genetic differences between human populations.

By a process of elimination, we are left with the conclusion that most group differences in population genotypes are the result of selection. Since selection acts by increasing the frequency of those genes that improve adaptation, we are further forced to the conclusion that genotypic differences in human populations represent adaptive responses to the environment.

This does not necessarily mean that the genotype of a group is adapted to the environment in which it is now found. Because of the long generation time for man and the rapid changes culture has produced in some aspects of his environment, a given gene may not have had any adaptive value to a population for several thousand years. Once the environment changed, the persistence of that particular gene would be governed purely by the intensity of selection against it and its dominance characteristics. The *sicklemia* gene found among American Negroes is an excellent example. Although it is clearly maladaptive in the recent environment of the American Negro, selection has not yet eliminated this gene, which was highly adaptive in the malarial environment of his forebears (Allison, 1955).

The conclusion that population differences in genotypes arose largely through selection also must not be viewed as proof that any given phenotypic characteristic of a group is or has been adaptive to an environment. As pointed out earlier, the human phenotype is almost always subject to environmental patterning through the various forms of genetic plasticity. Equally important, a specific gene can affect numerous phenotypic characteristics, while any individual phenotypic characteristic can have multiple gene determinants. Therefore, even when a close relationship exists between genetic inheritance and phenotypic characteristics, the adaptive value of the gene need not be related to any one aspect of the phenotype. Eye color is a good example. The exact inheritance pattern is not known, but it appears to be quite closely related to the genes involved in skin color variation. In such a situation, the variation in eye color and skin color may each have adaptive value, but it is equally possible that variation in only one of them has adpative value while the other tags along as a product of the multiple effects of the gene.

To end our discussion of evolutionary theory and genetic adaptation, we would like to suggest the following as a significant set of hypotheses to be tested.

1. Population differences in genotypes and gene frequencies are the product of environmental adaptation (including culture as a part of the environment).

2. The longer a population has lived in a set environment, the greater the probability that their genotypic eccentricities are a product of adaptation to that environment. Thus, *ecologically* stable populations will be more likely to show genetic adaptation than ecologically unstable ones, and genetic differences are more likely to be related to the stable stresses of the environment such as climate and disease than to the more changeable stresses such as those produced by culture.

3. Many phenotypic variations in man are not the product of genetic adaptation.

Evidence of Genetic Adaptation

When we turn from theory to the demonstrable evidence for genetic adaptation as a cause of population differences, the findings are thin. This does not necessarily imply a poor theory. Instead, it may at this time be attributed to (1) the relatively small number of studies that have been undertaken with the preceding hypotheses, and (2) our lack of knowledge concerning man's genetic system and the degree to which it is involved in man's enormous structural, functional, and behavioral diversity.

Each year a considerable number of new genes are identified in man, and very often they are found to be unequally distributed in human populations. This immediately suggests that they have some adaptive value in those populations where a high frequency exists. Occasionally, such an assumption is supported by strong presumptive evidence, such as the sicklemia-malaria chain (Allison, 1955). In other instances, as in the many links discovered between the abnormal hemoglobins and resistance to infectious disease, a direction for future research is indicated (Motulsky, 1960). However, for the majority of identified genes, even those such as the long-known genes underlying the ABO blood types, it is not yet possible to even suggest an acceptable adaptive explanation for frequency differences.

On the opposite side of the problem are the numerous traits that are obviously adaptive for the populations where they are found, but for which the genetic pathways are not known. Studies resulting from the newly rekindled interest in the sensory and physiological functioning of non-Western groups demonstrate an increasingly large variety of differences in human populations. While these differences are not of the magnitude that the nineteenth-century scientist conceived or the twentieth century "racist" imagines, the number is great and the differences are often of significant adaptive value to populations in their present or recently past environments. For this increasing list of traits, one of the major problems is differentiating how the responses relate to genetic variation and to adaptive plasticity. For example, it is quite clear that the warmer temperatures of the Eskimo hand when exposed to cold enhanced his adaptation to the environment in which he lived (Coffee, 1955). However, the extent of genetic causation in the warmer hand temperatures and degree to which different sources of biological adaptations are involved is not clear. It has been demonstrated that psychological accommodation to cold increases the temperature of the fingers when exposed to cold (Fox, 1963), presumably because anxiety is reduced by repeated exposures. It has also been shown that an acclimatization or training effect occurs, which further produces warmer hands by greater blood flow in most subjects (Egan, 1963). However, these factors do not appear to account for most of the variation. Yoshimura's and Iida's work (1952) showed that northern and southern Japanese have a difference in response after training, indicating there is also a developmental factor. Since American Negro and white soldiers, both from the south, manifest vastly different responses to cold stresses (Iampietro et al., 1959), while twins show a striking similarity in response (Meehan, 1955), one is also inclined to assume a genetic component even though no specific genes have been identified.

Actually, it would be most surprising if any specific genes were found associated with the differences in hand temperature upon exposure to extreme cold. From what is known of the mechanisms involved, gene action would be indirect, involving such links as hand size, the size of arterial *anastomoses*, forearm size and insulation, neural pathways, and even brain functions. When attempts at genetic analysis of these possible intermediates have been made, they have consistently yielded the same type of partial-genotype-causation answer. This is easily explainable by the multiple genes involved in producing each of these phenotypic characteristics, plus, of course, all the levels of plasticity.

As the preceding discussion has emphasized, evidence for genetic adaptation has been emanating from two sources, but the two sources are not, at this point, making a great deal of contact. On the one hand, we have genetic variation without known adaptive significance, and on the other, we have traits with obvious adaptive value for which the genetic basis is unknown. The geneticist wishing to test the hypothesis that genetic variation is the product of adaptation must untangle the known gene from its complex interrelationships with morphology, function, and behavior; the psychophysiologist or environmental physiologist has the equally difficult task of untangling behavior or function with demonstrable adaptive value from its environmental determinants to arrive at the genetic core. In these two lines of inquiry it is not surprising that the most conclusive cases have contained the simplest links. Thus, the adaptive nature of genotype and gene frequency variation have been best demonstrated between simply inherited hemoglobin types and the diseases that attack hemoglobin, and the best case for demonstrating a genetic component in adaptive behavior or function is where the function is closely associated with morphology, such as climate tolerance and body morphology (Hammel, 1964).

Probably the greatest danger to a fuller understanding of human adaptation comes from the very fact that these simple relationships are the easiest to establish. Thus, geneticists concentrate their efforts on the study of infectious disease, while the environmental physiologist concentrates on temperature. In such important environmental stress areas as nutrition, culture, sensory and motor requirements, altitude, and radiation, very few attempts have been made to link adaptive behavior and function to genetic factors. Yet, there is no reason to doubt that selection due to these forms of stress was at least as significant in producing genetic variation as was temperature and infectious disease.

BEHAVIORAL AND SOMATIC PLASTICITY AS ADAPTATION

It is surprising to find that despite extensive studies on man's adaptative capacity in the presence of stress, there is no commonly accepted terminology for differentiating the nature or the types of adaptive responses. If we use Prosser (1964) as a guide, physiologists would call the responses that enhance functioning in the presence of stress "adaptive responses"; and divide them into genetically determined responses called "adaptive variations" and environmentally induced responses called "acclimatization." The important point that geneticists would make here is that acclimatization responses are also built into the genetic structure; or, as Prosser states it, "the genotype determines the 'capacity' of an organism to adapt."

In the majority of psychological studies, an improvement in the human organism's adaptation to the environment is called adjustment, accommodation, or perhaps adaptation. If the word "acclimatization" appears, it is rare indeed. In the field of human growth and development, the language of the evolutionary geneticist or physiologist is even more alien; the studies of psychological development use the language of psychology, but the concept of physical growth as an adaptive process is so new that almost no terminology exists. The terminological problem may very well prevent the physiologist, psychologist, medical scientist, geneticist, and anthropologist from realizing that they often are involved in the study of very closely related facets of the same problem.

It was with the terminological confusion in mind that a three-way breakdown of adaptive phenotypic plasticity into psychological accommodation, physiological acclimatization, and developmental acclimatization was suggested earlier in this paper. It may be logically argued that there is no essential difference in the mechanisms that enhance adaptation in each of these three ways. All are based on the inherited plasticity of man; and all depend upon environmental stress, which feeds back through the human nervous system to enhance the functioning of the organism in the presence of a given stress. There is, perhaps, a time factor difference, since the three categories of adaptation require progressively longer developmental time. However, the major point is that whether one is studying the changes in pain threshold or the effect of altitude on the growth of human lungs, all may be viewed as part of man's enormous adaptive capacity and may be profitably considered within the framework of evolutionary adaptational theory.

Perhaps the most difficult aspect of studying phenotypic plasticity is the process of distinguishing between adaptive and maladaptive responses to stress. In most cases the critical question is "Adaptive to what?" The physiologist often has no problem. If he has exposed individuals to a high heat stress, then any response that reduces the strain on the temperature regulation system and enhances work performance is adaptive. On the other hand, it is not so clear to the psychologist that a reduction in the pain sensation with chronic exposure represents a reduction of strain, and he must still carefully define the situations in which it would enhance performance. For this reason, the psychologist has been quite sparing with the label "adaptive," and in sensory systems, such as hearing, a considerable difference of opinion is found on whether a given change in response to a sound should be called "masking," "fatigue," or "adaptation."

Most of this problem is not meaningful when the researcher is considering adaptive responses in relation to a specific stress. For a hungry hunter in the woods, identification of the sounds of a food animal among the many sounds of the forest is adaptive and would be fixed by evolution, whether or not it conforms to the psychologist's definition of fatigue, masking, or adaptation. Indeed, it appears that the precise reason why the terminology of adaptation is so confused is the lack of evolutionary and selection concepts in its usage by the psychophysiologist and even most other physiologists. Until very recent years, the search has been for the universal changes that improved performance or function. Individual differences were ignored when encountered, and the testing of different human populations was seldom attempted. This contrasts strangely with the psychology of tests and measurements in which consideration of the individual and group variation has been paramount, while the hopes of establishing the underlying reasons for the variation were minimal.

POPULATION VARIATION
IN ADAPTIVE RESPONSES

As noted in the section on genetic adaptation, two methods may be used to study population differences in adaptive capacity. The first involves relating known gene frequency variations in populations to the adaptive requirements of the environment. The second involves the actual measurement and comparison of the functional capacities of human populations in the presence of a given stress. Once a population difference in functional capacity has been established, we still have the difficult problem of sorting out genetic components from the sources of adaptation related simply to the different forms of plasticity; but first there must be the test for functional differences.

In those cases where functional differences have been investigated, the population differences have usually proved more substantial than anticipated. Thus, Motulsky (1960) showed that different populations show enormous differences in death rates from common infectious diseases. The environmental physiologist has also discovered quite a broad variation in population responses to physical environmental stresses such as temperature and altitude. Even in the area of nutrition it is now widely accepted that the nutritional needs of different human populations are not uniform (Grande, 1964).

Of course, knowledge in these areas is quite fragmentary, and often the adaptive significance of population variation is not apparent. Although the historical and travel literature is full of comments on the special sensory and motor skills of primitive populations, our scientific knowledge on the subject is negligible. The few studies that have been made suggest that there may be dramatic differences in the visual

(Mann, 1966) and auditory (Rosen et al., 1962) characteristics of different populations. We have essentially no knowledge about the possibilities of other sensory differences, or motor skills. I would not presume at this time to suggest that genetic differences exist; but I would be surprised if there were not significant population variations in many sensory and motor characteristics. Certainly, the testing of populations would be an important contribution to our knowledge of how human biological variability contributes to adaptation.

CONCLUSIONS

At this point many readers may feel that they have been exposed to a great deal of theory and generalities about how man's biological variation is related to his adaptive capacity but to very little firm data. The author is sympathetic with this view and refers the reader to *The Biology of Human Adaptability* (Baker and Weiner, 1966) for a survey of factual knowledge on this subject as viewed by geneticists and human biologists. *The Handbook of Physiology* section entitled "Adaptation to the Environment" (Dill, Adolph, and Wilbur, 1964) provides a comprehensive coverage from the viewpoint of physiology.

I have not attempted to summarize the data available for two major reasons: (1) the mass of material is too great for an article of this length; and (2) the information is too fragmentary to construct an overall pattern at this time. My purpose has been to provide a progress report on the scientific productivity of studying human biological variability as the product of adaptation in the evolutionary sense, and to present some of the meaningful questions to be asked and areas to be studied in the future.

Viewed in terms of an interim report, what conclusions can be reached? In my opinion, the following seem justified.

1. The concept that most genotypic differences in human populations are the result of adaptation to differing environments has emerged as a dominant theory.

2. The phenotypic variation in the behavior, physiological function, and morphology of human populations may very often have been "caused" by adaptation. Thus, the search for the causes of racial variation, of differences in the physiological and psychological functioning of groups, and even of cultural variations can be profitably pursued from the framework of evolutionary adaptation.

3. The phenotypic adaptations of man contain a high environmental patterning component. Thus, geneticists would do well to broaden the

base from which they search for genetic adaptation, while psychophysiologists and environmental physiologists would profit in their understanding of the sources of human adaptability by the design of studies that would allow the demonstration of developmental acclimatization and genetic adaptation.

Finally, I must note that popular questions such as whether race differences in intelligence exist, and if so, are they cultural or genetic in origin, are not meaningful questions at the present state of adaptational theory or evidence. At this time, we cannot even state with certainty the degree of genetic versus environmental patterning involved in the presumably adaptive variation in hand temperature; therefore, to debate seriously the genetic versus environmental patterning involved in man's total adaptive behavioral capacity (a common definition of intelligence) is inappropriate at this time as a scientific endeavor.

REFERENCES

Adams, R., and B. G. Covino. 1958. Racial variations to a standardized cold stress. *J. Appl. Physiol.* 12: 9–12.

Allison, A. C. 1955. Aspects of polymorphism in man. *Cold Spring Harbor Symp. Quant. Biol.* 20: 239–252.

Baker, P. T. 1958. Racial differences in heat tolerance. *Amer. J. Phys. Anthrop.* 16: 287–305.

Baker, P. T., and J. S. Weiner, eds. 1966. *The biology of human adaptability.* Oxford and New York: Oxford Univ. Press.

Coffee, M. F. 1955. A comparative study of young Eskimo and Indian males with acclimatized white males. In Ferrer, ed., *Cold injury.* New York: Josiah Macy, Jr. Foundation.

Dill, D. B., E. F. Adolph, and C. G. Wilbur, eds., 1964. *Handbook of physiology.* (Adaptation to the environment, Section 4.) Washington, D.C.: American Physiological Society.

Egan, C. J. 1963. Local vascular adaptations to cold in man. *Federation Proc.* 22: 547–551.

Fox, R. H. 1963. Comment following "Local vascular adaptations to cold in man" by C. J. Egan. *Federation Proc.* 22: 952.

Giles, E. 1965. Anthropological significance of recent New Guinea genetic studies. *Amer. J. Phys. Anthrop.* 23: 326.

Grande, F. 1964. Man under calorie deficiency. In D. B. Dill, E. F. Adolph, and C. G. Wilbur, eds., *Handbook of physiology.* (Adaptation to the environment. Section 4.) Washington, D.C.: American Physiology Society.

Hammel, T. H. 1964. Terrestial animals in cold: Recent studies of primitive man. In D. B. Dill, E. F. Adolph, and C. G. Wilbur, eds., *Handbook of physiology*. (Adaptation to the environment, Section 4.) Washington, D.C.: American Physiological Society.

Iampietro, P. F., R. F. Goldman, E. R. Buskirk, and D. E. Bass. 1959. Responses of Negro and white males to cold. *J. Appl. Physiol.* 14: 798–800.

Mann, Ida. 1966. *Culture, race, and climate and eye disease.* Springfield, Ill.: Charles C Thomas.

McCance, R. A., and W. M. B. Widdowson. 1951. The German background studies of undernutrition. Wuppertal, 1946-49. *Med. Res. Coun. Spec. Rep.* (London) 275: 1–20.

Meehan, J. P. 1955. Individual and racial variation in a vascular response to a cold stimulus. *Milit. Med.* 116: 330–334.

Monge, C. 1948. *Acclimatization in the Andes: Historical confirmation of "climate aggression" in the development of Andean man.* Baltimore: Johns Hopkins Press.

Motulsky, A. G. 1960. Metabolic polymorphisms and the role of infectious diseases in human evolution. In G. W. Lasker, ed., *The processes of ongoing human evolution*. Detroit: Wayne State Univ. Press.

Prosser, C. L. 1964. Perspectives of adaptation: Theoretical aspects. In D. B. Dill, E. F. Adolph, and C. G. Wilbur, eds., *Handbook of physiology*. (Adaptation to the environment, Section 4.) Washington, D.C.: American Physiological Society.

Rosen, S., M. Bergman, D. Plester, A. El. Mofty, and M. H. Satti. 1962. Presbycusis study of a relatively noise-free population in the Sudan. *Ann. Otol.* 71: 727–743.

Wright, S. 1943. Isolation by distance. *Genetics* 28: 114.

Yoshimura, H., and T. Iida. 1952. Studies on the reactivity of the skin vessels to extreme cold. Part 2: Factors governing individual reactivity on the resistance to frostbite. *Jap. J. Physiol.* 2: 177–185.

The rate of human growth and the pattern of development, like those of most biological traits, are the result of genetic and environmental interaction. Certain kinds of environmental factors have a predictable effect upon growth; but the extent of the effect depends in part upon the developmental state at which these influences are experienced and in part upon the inheritance of the individual. The growth-rate averages of populations, like those of individuals, differ. Rates of growth may be more rapid at an earlier age in one population than in another; this may or may not be compensated for in the second population by a later growth spurt. Differences such as these can probably be explained by both genetic and environmental factors, although thus far the role of environment has been easier to demonstrate. Also, such differences may vary in each of the various measures of growth: skeletal, dental, and sexual. Studies such as those on growth further emphasize how complex and variable the interrelationships can be between hereditary potential and environmental influences.

Ethnic Differences in Growth and Development

JEAN HIERNAUX
Centre de Biologie Humaine
Université Libre de Bruxelles
Brussels, Belgium

Like most biological traits, growth and development are controlled by the interaction of genes and environment. For a given trait, an individual inherits a range of possible values; his environment and his *genotype*[1] work together in determining the actual value within that range both during his growth span and adulthood. A short-term environmental disturbance will often produce a temporary variation in growth. In most cases, the depression caused by actual starvation or disease is soon compensated by catch-up growth (Tanner, 1963). However, there appears to be a period, centered on birth, during which starvation can induce long-term growth retardation and may stunt the adult size of males

---

[1]Words defined in the Glossary (p. 173) are italicized the first time they appear in each paper.

(Hiernaux, 1965). Environmental conditions during growth sometimes have an irreversible effect on adult physique; for example, one strain of mice develops a longer tail in a warm environment than it does at lower temperatures (Harrison, Hiorns, and Weiner, 1964). In Japan, a strong correlation has been demonstrated between adult stature and consumption of milk and eggs during childhood (Takahashi, 1966).

Populations, like individuals, differ in their rates of growth and development. Some of this variation may be caused by genetic factors within the groups. In assessing ethnic differences, we must be certain that a difference in growth is not entirely attributable to differences in the environment before assuming that it has a genetic component. Studies of genetically *similar* populations living in different environments and of genetically *different* populations living in similar environments are of great help in understanding such problems.

What are the population units to be compared for assessing ethnic differences? Experience has shown that the large "racial" classes like *Caucasoids, Negroids,* and *Mongoloids* do not suit the needs of studies of this type. In each of such large inclusive classes, the many genetic determinants of growth and physique may vary independently among the subpopulations found within each class.

The most suitable units for study are smaller local populations, groups of intermarrying persons, whether tribes, castes, or inhabitants of a particular region. Moreover, the group studied must be exposed to similar environmenal influences that have a differentiating effect on growth.

THE GROWTH PROCESS

We may see human growth as the process by which an individual reaches his adult size and shape from his initial one-cell state as a zygote or fertilized egg. Full adult stature is the end result, or target state, of this process. Individual or ethnic differences concern either the length of time taken for reaching it or the course followed, or both. Only *postnatal* growth will be considered here.

Skeletal, dental, and sexual development are the prime indicators of the growth process leading to *maturation*. All children do not mature at the same age, nor do the various indicators of maturation correlate perfectly. Skeletal and other *morphological* indicators of maturation are closely associated during adolescence with the age at *menarche* and development of secondary sex characters. On the other hand, the *deciduous teeth* appear to erupt quite independently of skeletal or bodily maturity. These various aspects of maturation will therefore be considered separately.

SKELETAL MATURATION

The stage of skeletal maturation of an individual is most commonly judged from an X-ray of the hand, by both the number of centers of *ossification* present and the degree of development of each. The skeletal age of the subject is judged from a set of standards for his population. The same variables are used to compare the tempo[2] of maturation in various populations.

Individual Variation

Individual variation in skeletal maturation is controlled by heredity, as is shown by the *correlation coefficients* between time of appearance of ossification centers in persons with varying degrees of relatedness. Unrelated persons shown no correlation, while identical twins, who are genetically identical because they derive from the same fertilized egg, are strongly similar in their timing of ossification (see Table 1).

Table 1. *Correlation coefficients between time of appearance of ossification centers in persons with varying degrees of relationship.*

Relationship	Correlation coefficient[a]
Identical twins	0.71
Siblings	0.28
First cousins	0.12
Unrelated	−0.01

Source. Data from Reynolds (1943) in Tanner (1962).

[a]A perfect correlation has a coefficient of 1; no correlation is represented by a coefficient of zero.

Environmental conditions also influence the tempo of skeletal maturation. Acheson and Fowler (1964) found British boys of higher socio-economic status maturing faster in their ossification than lower-class boys; this socioeconomic difference was less marked in girls. Tanner (1962) cites several papers based on experiments of starvation or *septi-*

---

[2]The word *tempo* as used throughout this article denotes the rhythm of development—the combination of rates and patterns of development.

caemia in rats showing that both conditions retard skeletal development. Unfortunately, few studies of human populations have been made to determine the extent of environmental influences on skeletal maturation rates.

Ethnic Differences

Many cases of ethnic differences in the tempo of skeletal development have been observed, some of which seem determined entirely by environment; for example, Greulich (1957) found that American-born children of Japanese origin are more similar to other Americans in tempo of ossification than they are to native Japanese children. Although Tanner (1966) feels that genetic differences are the cause of the advance in skeletal ossification observed at birth in several African populations, Massé (1965) considers the evidence for genetic causation inconclusive. She argues that much of the cause of advance is postnatal and may be explained by superior methods of infant care in some African populations. Ethnic differences in intrauterine conditons of life may be another factor, and Massé comments that differences in speed of embryonic development are known in man without a genetic causation having been proved. She cites a study by Scotland (1956) concluding that pregnancy is two weeks longer in East African women than in British or American women.

The faster rate of skeletal development displayed during the first months of life by some African populations is temporary as is the steeper rise of their height and weight curves during the same period. Comparing Dakar and American girls, Massé and Hunt (1963) observed that the growth spurt in Dakar girls ceases at eighteen months and from two years on American girls take the lead and maintain an advance of about one year in skeletal age. A similar difference between an African and an American population was found by Weiner and Thambipillai (1952) in comparing Accra and American school boys. From 9 to 17 years, Accra boys develop more slowly than Americans by an average of 16 months. The reversal in tempo of skeletal development and physical growth between Africans and Americans closely parallels that of their environmental history; the African enjoys superior nutritional and emotional conditions in infancy, but after that time the American has the greater environmental advantages.

From the data available today, we may conclude that thus far no genetic component has been definitely established for ethnic differences in tempo of skeletal maturation. However, environmental agents have been demonstrated in most of them.

DENTAL MATURATION

Dental maturation may be judged on the number of teeth erupted or on the presence or absence of a given tooth. By this data, an individual can be located on a scale for his population running from early to late maturers. By the use of graphs or by statistical methods, this information can be used to compare populations.

An individual's tempo of dental maturation is determined by both heredity and environment. As in skeletal maturation, the evidence for genetic control is best demonstrated by studies on twins. In rate of development of both deciduous and permanent teeth, twins or siblings resemble each other more closely than do unrelated persons growing up under similar conditions.

Environmental factors also influence the expression of heredity in dental maturation. In Germany, for example, Wurst (1964) observed that the permanent teeth of children of professional-level families erupt earlier than those of children of lower-level families. In North Slovakia, Valsik and Fábryová (1964) have noted an earlier eruption of permanent teeth associated with the general growth acceleration currently occurring in many European populations and in America. Higher standards of living are generally believed to play a role in this secular trend.

Factors internal to the mouth also influence tooth eruption. Fanning (1962) finds that the third molars erupt a year and a half earlier in children who have had a permanent tooth extracted in the same half-jaw.

Ethnic Differences

DECIDUOUS DENTITION. Tanner (1962) mentions that none of the studies showing an early advancement in skeletal maturation in African populations records a similar phenomenon for deciduous teeth. Although one study found deciduous teeth erupting earlier in a group of American Negroes than in American whites (Ferguson, Scott, and Bakwin, 1957), such a difference is not general in the United States according to the data compiled by Meredith (1946).

Table 2 gives the mean age of eruption of the deciduous lower first incisor, usually the first tooth to erupt, in several male populations. Environmental factors are evident in the differences, but no genetic component is conclusively established.

PERMANENT DENTITION. Data on median age at eruption of the permanent upper second molars in several male populations are given in Table 3. In three out of four African populations these molars erupt

Table 2. *Mean age of eruption of the deciduous lower first incisors, or of the first tooth, in various male populations.*

Population	Mean age (months)	Source
American Negro		
Private patients (Wash., D.C.)	6.2[a]	Ferguson, Scott, & Bakwin (1957)
Low-income families	8.3[a]	Rhoads et al. (1945) in Meredith (1946)
American white		
Private patients (New York)	6.8	Ferguson, Scott, & Bakwin (1957)
High-income families	7.3	Robinow et al. (1942) in Meredith (1946)
Hebrew Home (New York)	10.3[b]	Boas (1927) in Meredith (1946)
German (Munster)	7.9	Rhoads et al. (1945) in Meredith (1946)
Hutu (Rwanda)	7.8	Hiernaux and Vincke (unpublished)
Tutsi (Rwanda)	8.2	Hiernaux and Vincke (unpublished)

[a]Mean age for first tooth erupted. The mean age for eruption of lower first incisor would necessarily be older.

[b]Twenty days subtracted from the mean age published by Boas, who recorded only erupted teeth.

earlier than in any European or American white sample, but the difference is less than a year between the earliest maturing African and English groups. The fourth African group, the Tutsi, falls within the range of the English and American populations.

We need to know more about environmental factors in tooth eruption to make a valid interpretation of these data. Space available on the jaws is surely a factor. MacKay and Martin (1952) note that deciduous teeth decay earlier in Digo than in British children; this early loss could be partly responsible for the earlier eruption of the permanent teeth in the Digo. Probably the best documented difference is that between the Tutsi and Hutu. They live side by side, but the Tutsi's diet is richer in milk, and hence in calcium and proteins, during childhood. Nonetheless, in the Tutsi the second molars erupt later, which would seem to indicate a genetic difference, though not necessarily one directly controlling the

Table 3. *Median age at eruption of permanent upper second molars in various populations.*

Population	Median age (years)
Digo (Kenya)	11.3[a]
Pima Indians (U.S.A.)	11.4
Zulu (South Africa)	11.7
Hutu (Rwanda)	11.9[b]
Tutsi (Rwanda)	12.2[b]
English	
Sample 1	12.0
Sample 2	12.3
American whites	
Sample 1	12.2
Sample 2	12.7
Sample 3	12.8

Source. Data from Dahlberg and Menegaz-Bock (1958) unless otherwise indicated.
  [a]MacKay and Martin (1952).
  [b]Hiernaux (1965).

rate of dental development. It may be an indirect genetic causation in that their later tooth eruption may be due to their genetically narrower jaws (Hiernaux, 1965).

The available data on the eruption of the third permanent molars show no systematic difference in tempo between populations of the various continents (Hiernaux, 1965). Tutsi from Rwanda and Wolof from Dakar are later maturers than Americans, while the Hutu are approximately on a par with Americans. The Digo and the Zulu are earlier maturers than the Hutu while the Czechs seem to be later.

Dahlberg and Menegaz-Bock (1958) observed that Pima Indian children in Arizona erupt their permanent front teeth later than English children, but their permanent back teeth earlier. Tanner (1962) summarizes their findings as follows: "Possibly these differences, or some of them, are genetical in origin, but an alternative explanation is available in the case of the posterior teeth. Pima children experience, it is said, a much greater degree of wear and tear on their deciduous molars than do English children, and there is some evidence that this may cause earlier shedding. There is also some evidence that extraction of a deciduous tooth causes an earlier appearance of the corresponding permanent one, so that early shedding might actually cause earlier eruption."

In dental as in skeletal maturation, there is no conclusive evidence of a genetic component in ethnic differences.

SEXUAL MATURATION

Menarche, or onset of the first menses, offers an excellent indicator of sexual maturation of females. The gradual development of secondary sex characters, such as pubic hair and breasts in girls, and beard in boys, does not offer the ease of recording a "present or absent" phenomenon that menstruation does. The age of a girl at menarche may be compared to the standard for her population, or median values of this age may be compared in different populations. Since boys reach puberty later than girls by a time interval that does not seem to vary considerably between populations, age at menarche permits us to estimate interpopulation differences in tempo of sexual maturation for both sexes.

Individual Variation

Here again, the influence of heredity is demonstrated by the contrast between female twins and women of different degrees of relatedness (Table 4). The effect of environmental factors on age at menarche is also amply demonstrated. Socioeconomic standing, which affects nutrition and hygiene, is one of these factors (see Table 5). Graffar and Corbier (1965) cite studies showing that a temporary deterioration in living conditions delays puberty. The increase in age at maturation observed

Table 4. *Mean difference in age at menarche between women of decreasing degree of relationship.*

Relationship	Difference (months)
Identical twins	2.8
Fraternal twins	12.0
Sisters	12.9
Unrelated women	18.6

Source. Data from Petri (1935) in Tanner (1962).

Table 5. *Median age at menarche by socioeconomic status.*

Population	Median age (years)	
	High status	*Low status*
Chinese (Hong Kong)	12.5	13.3
Bantu (Transkei)	15.0	15.4

Source. Data from Tanner (1966).

during World War II in Belgium, France, and Germany was as much as two years in some places. The same phenomenon was noted in Hagerstown, Maryland, during the economic depression of the 1930s. Age at menarche clearly manifests a greater sensitivity to living conditions than does dental eruption.

Another factor acting on the age at menarche is family size, puberty being later in larger-sized families. Again this seems to be essentially socioeconomic in nature. Family size has been shown to influence the rate of physical maturation as well as that of sexual maturation, and it also conditions adult size (members of larger families tending to be shorter in stature).

Puberty is generally later in rural than in urban areas. Three examples, drawn from Tanner (1966), are given in Table 6. The environmental factors implied in this difference are hard to define. Nutrition, hygiene, and intensity of sensorial stimulation have all been suggested. The possibility of genetic differences between urban and rural populations, and

Table 6. *Median age at menarche in urban and rural areas.*

Country	Median age (years)	
	Urban	*Rural*
Ceylon	12.8	14.4
U.S.S.R.	13.0	14.3
Rumania	13.5	14.6

Source. Data from Tanner (1966).

also between social classes, cannot be dismissed as a partial basis for the differences in tempo of maturation.

Altitude may also delay puberty. Wurst (1962) observed a later menarche at higher altitude in Austria, but he attributes it to the hard physical labor required of adolescents in the area. Valsik, Stukovsky, and Bernatova (1963) observed a similar retardation in Czechoslovakia of three months for each hundred meters of added altitude. Here again, it is not certain that altitude is the conditioning factor, since nutrition was poorer at higher altitudes.

Some authors have considered climate to be an important influence on age at menarche. For example, Mills (1950) stated that girls and animals both show a delayed onset of the menses and retarded growth in prolonged heat. However, a comparison between populations living in hot and in cold areas does not demonstrate any correlation between climate and age at menarche (Tanner, 1962).

Ethnic Differences

The range of median ages at menarche in present-day populations is large, extending from 12.3 to 18.8 years. Table 7 gives a selection of the known values. Mills's hypothesis that menarche is delayed by heat is not supported by the data; the earliest maturing populations live in hot climates, while the latest maturers in Africa live in a fairly temperate climate in Rwanda. Similarly, there is no evidence that earlier maturation occurs in warmer countries; for example, the age at menarche is identical in Moscow and Tel Aviv.

No clean genetic difference between continents is evident. All five African populations represented are relatively late maturers, but Cuban Negroes are the earliest maturers. The three earliest ages are displayed by a Negro, a white, and a Chinese group. In both studies made in Cuba, the difference between Negroes, whites, and mulattoes proved to be insignificant.

Tanner (1966) suspects the genetic threshold may be lower for Chinese than for English, and perhaps also lower for East Europeans than for West Europeans. More data on genetically diverse populations living in a variety of environments is necessary for either substantiating or ruling out this hypothesis. For the time being, all we can do is to consider the possible determinants of age at menarche; for example, the late puberty in Rwanda could be due to the cumulative effect of relatively poor nutrition, *endemic diseases*, rurality, altitude, and a genetic component as well (Hiernaux, 1965). We must also keep in mind the fact that this lateness by reference to Europe is a recent development; a

Table 7. *Median age at menarche in several populations.*

Population or location	Median age (years)
Cuba	
Negro	12.4
White	12.4
Mulatto	12.6
Cuba	
Negro	12.9[a]
White	13.0[a]
Mulatto	13.0[a]
Hong Kong (wealthy Chinese)	12.5
Florence, Italy	12.5
Wroclaw, Poland	12.6
Budapest, Hungary	12.8
California, U.S.A.	12.8
Colombo, Ceylon	12.8
Moscow, U.S.S.R.	13.0
Tel Aviv, Israel	13.0[b]
London, U.K.	13.1
Assam, India (city dwellers)	13.2
Burma (city dwellers)	13.2
Uganda (wealthy Kampala)	13.4
Oslo, Norway	13.5
France	13.5
Nigeria (wealthy Ibo)	14.1
U.S.S.R. (rural Buriats)	15.0
South Africa (Transkei Bantu)	15.0
Rwanda	
Tutsi	16.5[c]
Hutu	17.1[c]
New Guinea (Bundi)	18.8

Source. Data from Tanner (1966) unless otherwise indicated.

[a]Pospisilova-Zuzakova, Stukovsky, and Valsik (1965)
[b]Ber and Brociner (1964).
[c]Hiernaux (1965).

century ago, age at menarche in Norway was similar to that in Rwanda today (Tanner, 1966).

Since some studies indicate a tendency for late maturers to be taller (Tanner, 1962), it would be easy to postulate that certain populations owe their tall stature to a constitutionally late maturation. However, there is no direct evidence for such a causation. In Rwanda, male Tutsi grow taller than Hutu by 10 cm on the average, while maturing a little earlier; the difference in adult stature results from higher increments in the Tutsi along the entire growth span (Hiernaux, 1965). The trend towards earlier maturation observed in recent times in several parts of the world is accompanied by a trend towards taller statures. For the time being, there is no firm evidence that the timing of sexual maturation is related to ethnic differences in adult stature.

GROWTH SPURTS

Puberty is characterized in both sexes by a growth spurt in height. Age at menarche, like that of adolescent development of the penis and the male secondary sex characters, is highly correlated with the onset, peak, and termination of the growth spurt, and also with the percentage of adult stature attained. Since postadolescent growth rapidly falls to nearly zero, age at cessation of growth is closely correlated with age at puberty.

Preadolescent growth is not uniform in rate. However, growth in fat, estimated by the thickness of skinfolds, shows a marked growth spurt about six to seven years before puberty in females, and cross-sectional studies are revealing about differences between groups. In English girls, growth curves for triceps skinfold rise at 6.5 years, continuing upward to adulthood, with a step at 10.5–11.5 years (see Tanner, 1964). The influence of environment on this growth spurt is shown by the data of Fry et al. (1965) on Chinese girls in Hong Kong; the increase occurs at 6, 7, and 8 years in high, middle, and low socioeconomic groups respectively. Few ethnic groups have yet been compared for this phenomenon. The rise occurs a half year earlier in Polish girls (Wolanski, 1962) than in the English. In the male sex also, it occurs earlier in Poland than in England, at 6 years compared to 7.5 years. On the other hand, Sara girls in Southern Chad had not yet experienced this growth spurt by the age of 11, the latest age class studied (Asnes, unpublished).

We must wait for more data before trying to interpret ethnic differences in this trait. There is an indication that its individual variation is partly controlled by heredity, involving, in girls at least, a constitutional association between high body weight relative to stature at 7 years, early puberty, and high adult relative weight (Tanner, 1962). Perhaps the Poles, who show an advance on the English both in sexual maturation and a growth spurt in fat, partly owe this difference to a higher frequency in the population of a genetic predisposition to early fat accumulation and puberty.

GROWTH AND ETHNIC DIFFERENCES IN ADULT BODILY PROPORTIONS

Physical anthropologists are unceasingly adding new cases of ethnic differences in adult body proportions. A large number of them undoubtedly have a genetic component. Since adult proportions result from the growth of the variables concerned, it is of interest to know at which period of growth and by which modalities ethnic differences in proportions do develop. Mann et al. (1962) put forth the hypothesis that the small stature of the African Pygmies results from an early cessation of growth; but the uncertainty about the age of the Pygmy children makes the evidence for this hypothesis little reliable.

In Rwanda, the growth of Tutsi and Hutu boys was compared. While living in roughly similar environmental conditions, they attain quite different adult physiques. A comparison, therefore, essentially reveals how genetic differences in proportions develop. For the relationship between hip width and stature, the genetic difference between the Tutsi and Hutu manifests itself late, by a divergent curve following a long, practically common segment. From the point of divergence on, the Hutu accelerate their growth in hip width relative to growth in height, while the Tutsi boys decelerate it (Figure 1). The Hutu curve runs parallel to the one for American white boys, who show much wider hips relative to stature at all ages. Figure 1 demonstrates that genetically different populations may reach their adult proportions through different growth processes. This is an area still barely touched by physical anthropology.

HETEROSIS AND GROWTH

Experimentation on animals and plants has shown that crossing two different strains of a species often produces an offspring that is more vigorous than either parental strain. This phenomenon is called *heterosis* or hybrid vigor. It seems related to the increase in the *heterozygosity* of

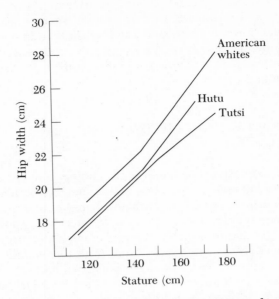

Figure 1. *Major axes of the relation between hip width and stature of males from 6 years on in American whites, Hutu, and Tutsi.*

the hybrids. A similar phenomenon has been observed in man when the isolation of small inbred communities is disturbed, resulting in a lower proportion of *homozygotes* in the population. In at least some instances, heterosis seems capable of increasing adult stature by 2 cm in one generation (Hulse, 1957). To change adult stature, heterosis has necessarily influenced growth.

Schull (1962) observed a depression of physical growth in Japanese children of *consanguineous* parents. He also observed a more vigorous growth in children whose parents were not related but were themselves offspring of consanguineous matings. Both observations suggest heterosis.

We might expect to find some evidence of heterosis in growth curves of groups of individuals whose parents belong to genetically different populations. Very few studies have been published on this point so far. There is some evidence that heterosis may be responsible for a later weight increase during growth in a group of Franco-Vietnamese children (Hiernaux and Heintz, 1967). Effects of heterosis on the adult size of members of newly mixed populations is hardly more documented.

Benoist (1963) concludes that the adult stature of the Martinique population displays some degree of it. This population is still in the process of genetic homogenization of its two main historical components, African and European.

SUMMARY

The tempo of skeletal, dental, and sexual maturation may vary among individuals and among populations. Both heredity and environment have been shown to play a role in individual variation. The role of environment in interpopulational variation has been amply demonstrated; genetic differences between populations in tempo of maturation have not been proved; but the possibility that they exist has not been ruled out either.

REFERENCES

Acheson, R. M., and C. B. Fowler. 1964. Sex, socio-economic status, and secular increase in stature. A family study. *Brit. J. Prev. Soc. Med.* 18: 25–33.

Benoist, J. 1963. Les Martiniquais. Anthropologie d'une population métissée. *Bull. Mém. Soc. Anthrop. Paris.* 11: 241–432.

Ber, A., and C. Brociner. 1964. Age of puberty in Israeli girls. *Fert. Steril.* 15: 640–647.

Dahlberg, A. A., and R. M. Menegaz-Bock. 1958. Emergence of the permanent teeth in Pima Indian children. A critical analysis of method and an estimate of population parameters. *J. Dent. Res.* 37: 1123–1140.

Fanning, E. A. 1962. Third molar emergence in Bostonians. *Amer. J. Phys. Anthrop.* 20: 339–345.

Ferguson, A. D., R. B. Scott, and H. Bakwin. 1957. Growth and development of Negro infants. VIII. Comparison of the deciduous dentition in Negro and white infants (a preliminary study). *J. Pediat.* 50: 327–331.

Fry, E. I., K. S. F. Chang, M. M. C. Lee, and C. K. Ng. 1965. The amount and distribution of subcutaneous tissue in southern Chinese children from Hong Kong. *Amer. J. Phys. Anthrop.* 23: 69–80.

Graffar, M., and J. Corbier. 1965. Influence des facteurs socioéconomiques. *20e Congrés des Pédiatres de Langue Francaise* (Nancy). Vol. II, pp. 127–155.

Greulich, W. W. 1957. A comparison of the physical growth and development of American-born and native Japanese children. *Amer. J. Phys. Anthrop.* 15: 489–515.

Harrison, G. A., R. W. Hiorns, and J. S. Weiner. 1964. The growth of mice in a fluctuating temperature environment. *Proc. Roy. Soc. Brit.* 160: 138–148.

Hiernaux, J. 1965. *La croissance des écoliers Rwandais.* Roy. Acad. Sci., Outre-Mer, Brussels.

Hiernaux, J., and N. Heintz. 1967. Croissance biométrique des Franco-Vietnamiens. *Bull. Mém. Soc. Anthrop. Paris.* 7: 55–89.

Hulse, F. S. 1957. Exogamie et hétérosis. *Arch. Suiss. Anthrop. Géner.* 22: 103–125.

MacKay, D. H., and W. J. Martin. 1962. Dentition and physique of Bantu children. *J. Trop. Med. Hyg.* 55: 265–275.

Mann, G. V., O. A. Roels, D. L. Price, and J. M. Merril. 1962. Cardiovascular disease in African pygmies. *J. Chron. Dis.* 15: 341–371.

Massé, G., and E. E. Hunt. 1963. Skeletal maturation of the hand and wrist in West African children. *Hum. Biol.* 35: 1–25.

Massé, G. 1965. Croissance et facteurs ethniques. *20e Congrés des Pédiatres de Langue Francaise* (Nancy). Vol. II, pp. 159–180.

Meredith, H. V. 1946. Order and age of eruption for the deciduous dentition *J. Dent. Res.* 25: 43–66.

Mills, C. 1950. Temperature influence over human growth and development. *Hum. Biol.* 22: 71–74.

Pospisilova-Zuzakova, V., R. Stukovsky, and J. A. Valsik. 1965. The menarche in whites, Negresses, and mulatto women of Havana. *Z. Arztl. Fortbild.* (Jena) 59: 500–516.

Scotland, W. H. D. 1956. Length of gestation of East African women. *J. Obstet. Gynaec. Brit. Emp.* 63: 120–123.

Schull, W. J. 1962. Inbreeding and maternal effects of the Japanese. *Eugen. Quart.* 5: 14–22.

Takahashi, E. 1966. Growth and environmental factors in Japan. *Hum. Biol.* 38: 112–130.

Tanner, J. M. 1962. *Growth at adolescence,* 2nd ed. Oxford: Blackwell.

Tanner, J. M. 1963. The regulation of human growth. *Child Dev.* 34: 817–847.

Tanner, J. M. 1964. Human growth and constitution. In G. A. Harrison, J. S. Weiner, J. M. Tanner, and N. A. Barnicot, eds., *Human biology.* Oxford and New York: Oxford Univ. Press.

Tanner, J. M. 1966. The secular trend towards earlier physical maturation. *Trans. Soc. Geneesk,* 44: 524–538.

Valsik, J. A., R. Stukovsky, and L. Bernatova. 1963. Quelques facteurs géographiques et sociaux ayant une influence sur l'age de la puberté. *Biotypologie.* 23: 109–121.

Valsik, J. A., and E. Fábryová, 1964. Einige Beobachtungen uber die Eruption der bleibenden Zahne in der Nordslowakei. *Deut. Stomatol.* 14: 263–274.

Weiner, J. S., and V. Thambipillai. 1952. Skeletal maturation of West African Negroes. *Amer. J. Phys. Anthrop.* 10: 407–418.

Wolanski, N. 1962. *Kinetyka i dynamika roswoju fizycznego dzieci i mlodziezy.* Panstwowy Zaktad Wydawnictu Lekarsckich, Warsaw.

Wurst, F. 1962. Beruf der Eltern und Wohnstatte in ihren Einfluss auf die korperliche und geistige Entwicklung des Kindes. *Z. Artzl. Fortbild.* 55: 211–214.

Wurst, F. 1964. *Umweltseinflusse auf Wachstum und Entwicklung. Stadt und Landkinder in Kornten.* J. A. Barch.

Disease has been a major selective factor in human evolution, and racial or ethnic groups differ in many of the diseases to which they are either susceptible or relatively resistive. The existence of these differences is of great assistance in discovering the causation of certain types of disease, and is even an aid in the management or prevention of many diseases. No racial group is free of its own distinctive pattern of disease, and, consequently, no group can be considered either pathological or free of pathology. Studies of group differences in disease is neither racist nor discriminatory, but rather serves to benefit the health care of all people.

Race, Ethnic Group and Disease

ALBERT DAMON
Department of Anthropology
Harvard University
Cambridge, Massachusetts

The associations between disease and racial or ethnic group concern a variety of scientists and administrators. The practicing physician can use such information in the diagnosis and treatment of disease; the public health official, in planning programs which aim to detect, prevent, or eradicate disease, as well as in allocating scarce and costly health resources like doctors, nurses, educators, clinics, and hospitals. The epidemiologist uses such data to help explain the distribution and determinants of disease frequency, thereby suggesting leads for the laboratory scientist's investigation of the causes of disease. The demographer uses knowledge of the racial distribution of disease to help explain distinctive patterns of population structure of vital statistics.

Among basic scientists, the geneticist deals with the mechanisms and mode of transmission of hereditary disease within populations and with the differing gene frequencies among populations separated in time, place, and origin. The anthropologist tries to account for such population differences in terms of the origin, evolution, distribution, and differing environments—natural, biological, and cultural—of the populations concerned. Disease is a major selective factor in human *evolution*,[1] and

---

[1]Words defined in the Glossary (p. 173) are italicized the first time they appear in each paper.

its present distribution affords clues to the past history and future course of mankind.

The difference between the approaches of the basic and the applied human biologist is that the former attempts to explain human variation. He regards the manifestations of human diversity as the dependent variable—dependent on climate, habitat, migration, inbreeding, and genetic mechanisms. The applied scientist, on the other hand, takes the manifestations of human variability as given—that is, as the independent variable—and tries to turn these biological differences to practical ends, such as finding, treating, and preventing disease.

Before presenting the associations between race and disease, let us define some terms. The science of the distribution and determinants of disease in man is epidemiology, an applied biomedical discipline that has recently expanded its scope from infectious disease ("epidemics") to the chronic, noninfectious disorders of multiple or uncertain etiology which now account for most of the disability and deaths in advanced societies. Examples are coronary heart disease, hypertension, cancer, "strokes," arthritis, peptic ulcer, and mental illness.

As in other observational sciences, the first step in epidemiologic method (MacMahon, Pugh, and Ipsen, 1960) is description. The prevalence of disease is charted in respect to time, place, and person. The personal or "host" characteristics most relevant to disease frequency are age, sex, and race. Of secondary importance, on the whole, are other biological traits like physical constitution, birth order and maternal age, and socioeconomic traits like income, occupation, and marital status. Sometimes, as for single-gene disorders like *hemophilia*, genetic constitution is of prime importance.

From his initial description the epidemiologist frames hypotheses to account for the observed distributions. He then tests these hypotheses by specifically designed quantitative, analytic studies, still observational in method. If his hypothesis survives analytic test, his final step is to clinch the proof by experiment—as, for example, in fluoridating water supplies to reduce caries frequency.

It can be seen that clinical medicine, pathology, physical anthropology, and demography all contribute to descriptive epidemiology. Our concern here is with the personal characteristic of race—a concept of physical anthropology—in its association with disease, as defined clinically and pathologically. We shall summarize the evidence briefly and then discuss possible explanations. Fortunately, the only strong emotion aroused by this aspect of race is humanitarian, to prevent or relieve suffering, so that we need not plead to justify the research or debate the ethics of examining the evidence.

DEFINITION OF RACE AND ETHNIC GROUP

For descriptive purposes, the epidemiologist analyzes disease rates among groups of persons who are more homogeneous than the general population, whether this relative homogeneity has been derived biologically or culturally. The word "relative" should be stressed, both because human beings and human groups, like all living things, are innately variable and because no group is completely isolated from outside influence. A *biologically* distinct group can be termed a race or population. Such a group, as a result of past breeding patterns, has a "relatively" large percentage of genes in common. The great preponderance of human genes are, of course, shared by all men. A racial group may vary in number from a few hundred to a few hundred million, and in residential area, whether of origin or of current residence, from local to geographic to continental in size (Garn, 1965).

A racial group may, and in fact often does, have distinguishing physical features—like skin color, hair form, and facial conformation—as well as distinctive aggregates of genes (*genotype*) and of traits (*phenotype*) determined by laboratory test but not externally apparent. Examples of such cryptic genetic traits are blood groups, *hemoglobin* variants, blood cell and serum *enzymes*, and ability to taste *phenylthio-carbamide*.

A *culturally* distinct group is an ethnic group. Frequently the two kinds of homogeneity, biological and cultural, overlap or coincide, as in the case of most primitive tribes or of linguistic, religious, or colored minorities in a city or country, provided only that the members of the group share a common ancestry. For many practical purposes then, including epidemiologic description, it may not matter *how* a particular group under study became distinctive, nor the precise proportion of biology and culture in its present distinctiveness. The Boston Irish, Italian, Jewish, Armenian, and Negro communities, for example, are distinctive both biologically and culturally; they are racial as well as ethnic groupings.

Biological and cultural similarity can reinforce one another. On the one hand, distinctive physical features make it easy for society to practice or enforce certain breeding patterns, as intermarriage or interbreeding between white persons and Negroes is now forbidden in South Africa. On the other hand, distinctive cultural practices like religion may isolate breeding populations more or less completely, as in the case of the Jews for many centuries, or small contemporary groups like the Amish, Dunkers, and Hutterites. Whatever has caused or continues to maintain a group in relative isolation, social or biological, the net result is a group with more genes or social practices, or both, in common than the population at large.

It is important to distinguish between biological and cultural homogeneity in investigating the cause of disease or in attempting prevention. In the case of genetic diseases occurring mainly or exclusively among groups which may be both racial and ethnic, it would be fruitless to seek explanation in terms of current cultural practices. Whatever the cultural or environmental factors at the origin of or contributing to the persistence of the hemoglobin S (*sickle-cell*) mutation among African Negroes or Tay-Sachs disease (infantile amaurotic idiocy) among Jews, the current bearers of these genes are defined biologically, not culturally. On the other hand, one should not ascribe differences in disease frequency to racial or biological homogeneity unless cultural and environmental factors can be ruled out. For all human diseases, both heredity and environment are involved, the relative proportions varying from one disease, population, and person to another.

RACE AND DISEASE

For a general picture, let us first examine racial differences in disease within a single country, the United States. Here, medical diagnosis and population coverage, though by no means perfect, are more uniform for the various racial and ethnic subgroups than would be the case in international comparisons. There are three major *indices* of health or disease status for a population or group: mortality as reflected by death certification, examination of a representative sample, and morbidity (illness) as measured by household or hospital surveys. We shall consider only the first two, since hospital records and household interviews correspond poorly with the true medical status of a population.

Mortality in the United States

In the 1960 census, whites made up 88.6% of the population of 179,326,000, and nonwhites 11.4%. The nonwhites were 92% of Negro, 2.6% American Indian, 2.3% Japanese, 1.2% Chinese, 0.9% Filipino, and 1.1% all others. Needless to say, the "whites" were also ethnically and biologically diverse, as will be discussed below. Mortality rates for whites and nonwhites in 1900 and 1965 appear in Table 1. In both years the nonwhite death rates exceeded those for whites. Despite the great reduction in death rates since 1900, 60% among whites and 63% among

Table 1. *Death rates for whites and nonwhites in the United States, 1900 and 1965 (annual rates per 1,000 population in specified group).*

Year	Mortality rates				Rate in whites as percentage of rate in nonwhites	
	Whites		Nonwhites			
	Unadjusted	Adjusted[a]	Unadjusted	Adjusted[a]	Unadjusted	Adjusted[a]
1900	17.0	17.6	25.0	27.8	68	63
1965	9.4	7.1	9.6	10.3	98	69

[a]Adjusted to the age distribution of the total U.S. population in 1940, to take account of age differences and changes in the white and nonwhite populations.

nonwhites, the relative proportions (adjusted for age) have moved only slightly toward equality. A further breakdown by age, omitted here, shows 1965 mortality rates for nonwhites higher at all ages except 75 and over.

More informative is the comparison of death rates by cause, set out in Table 2. On the whole, the white rates exceeded nonwhite rates in the chronic, noninfectious, and "degenerative" diseases, with the major exceptions of *diabetes*, hypertension, and "strokes" (vascular lesions of the central nervous system), which are associated with hypertension. The nonwhites, on the other hand, had higher death rates for infectious diseases and genital cancer. With the sole exception of genital cancer, white cancer rates were higher. Among subcategories of cancer not shown in Table 2, white death rates were four to five times higher than nonwhite rates for testicular and skin cancer, roughly equal for prostatic and endometrial cancer, but only 50% and 67% as high as nonwhite rates for cervical and penile cancer, respectively.

National Health Examination Survey

Data from this survey, conducted between 1962 and 1964 on 6,672 adults aged 18 to 79 years and representing the civilian, noninstitutionalized population of the United States, can tell only about common morbid conditions. One would hardly expect such a small sample to contain many persons with cancer, for example. For the same reason—small numbers in the total sample—the nonwhites were virtually all Negroes.

The major finding relevant to race and disease are these. White and Negro rates were similar for coronary heart disease, rheumatoid arthri-

Table 2. *Death rates from selected causes for whites and nonwhites in the United States, 1965 (per 100,000 population in specified group).*

Cause	Mortality rates		Rate in whites as percentage of rate in nonwhites
	Whites	Nonwhites	
Suicide	11.9	5.0	238
Leukemia	7.4	4.1	180
Arteriosclerotic heart disease	303.8	175.8	173
Urinary cancer	7.5	4.6	163
Lymphosarcoma	8.1	5.1	159
Breast cancer	14.6	9.5	154
Peptic ulcer	5.6	3.8	147
Respiratory cancer	27.7	20.6	134
Digestive cancer	49.6	41.8	119
Motor vehicle accidents	25.3	25.8	98
Vascular lesions of the central nervous system	102.3	114.7	89
Genital cancer	20.5	23.3	88
Cirrhosis of liver	12.5	14.6	86
Diabetes mellitus	16.7	20.1	83
Accidents, other than motor vehicle	28.9	41.2	70
Pneumonia	28.9	44.2	65
Hypertensive heart disease	24.7	55.3	45
Tuberculosis	3.4	9.3	37
Syphilis	1.0	2.8	36
Homicide	3.0	24.6	12

tis, and osteoarthritis. Negro rates were significantly higher for hypertension; for hypertensive heart disease, both absolutely and as a percentage of those with hypertension; and for syphilis, as indicated by positive serological test. Negroes had superior hearing and (uncorrected) visual acuity, for both near and distant vision. Negroes had higher mean blood pressure levels, both systolic and diastolic, than whites. Negro men had higher blood glucose and lower cholesterol levels than white men. Negroes of both sexes had only two-thirds as many decayed, missing, and filled teeth as whites, even among persons of the same income or education. On the other hand, Negroes had one and a half times the periodental (gum) disease of whites.

Special Surveys

Data for other nonwhites in the United States are sparse, being confined, among American Indians as a whole, to infectious diseases and accidents, both of which show higher than national rates (Wagner and Rabeau, 1964), or to surveys of specific conditions. For example, osteoarthritis is relatively frequent among Blackfoot and Pima Indians; diabetes, among the Papago; and gallbladder disease, trachoma, and congenitally dislocated hips among Southwestern Indians in general. On the other hand, Southwestern Indians have relatively little duodenal ulcer (Sievers and Marquis, 1962) despite a high percentage of Indians (83% or more) with blood group O, which is associated with duodenal ulcer among Caucasians, Japanese, and Nigerians.

On Hawaii, persons of pure or predominantly Polynesian ancestry have strikingly high rates of diabetes (Sloan, 1963). For coronary heart disease, their rates exceed those among Caucasians, Filipinos, and Japanese living in Hawaii (Moellering and Bassett, 1967). Rates were higher for pure Hawaiians than for part Hawaiians. Among men with coronary heart disease, Hawaiians were three times as likely to die from the acute episode as Japanese, and pure Hawaiians were more likely to die than part Hawaiians.

Chinese and Japanese in the United States show some distinctive patterns, particularly in respect to cancer. Among both groups, death rates for prostatic cancer and breast cancer are much lower than for the white population, and rates for digestive cancer (esophagus, stomach, and liver) much higher. The Japanese have unusually high rates for esophageal and stomach cancer as do the Chinese for nasopharyngeal and liver cancer (Smith, 1956a, b). In both groups, chronic lymphatic *leukemia* is about half as common as among the white population (Shimkin and Loveland, 1961).

The number of such comparisons could be greatly extended within other countries having distinctive racial and ethnic groups, such as South Africa and Israel, as well as in the United States. Tables 3 and 4, the former and part of the latter from McKusick (1967), summarize the associations between race or ethnic group and disease for simply inherited disorders (Table 3) and for disorders of complex genetics or

Table 3.   *Racial and ethnic disease: simply inherited disorders.*

Ethnic group	Relatively high frequency	Relatively low frequency

Ashkenazic Jews	Abetalipoproteinemia
	Bloom's disease
	Dystonia musculorum
	  deformans
	Factor XI (PTA) deficiency
	Familial dysautonomia
	Gaucher's disease
	Niemann-Pick disease
	Pentosuria
	Spongy degeneration of
	  brain
	Stub thumbs
	Tay-Sachs disease
		Phenylketonuria

Mediterranean peoples
  (Greeks, Italians,
  Sephardic Jews)
	Familial Mediterranean fever
	G-6-PD deficiency,
	  Mediterranean type
	Thalassemia (mainly β)
		Cystic fibrosis

Africans	G-6-PD deficiency, African
	  type
	Hemoglobinopathies, esp.
	  Hb S, Hb C, α and β thal,
	  persistent Hb F
		Cystic fibrosis
		Hemophilia
		Phenylketonuria
		Wilson's disease

Japanese (Koreans)	Acatalasia Dyschromatosis universalis hereditaria Oguchi's disease	
Chinese	α thalassemia G-6-PD deficiency, Chinese type	
Armenians	Familial Mediterranean fever	

Source.   Data from McKusick, 1967. For references on individual conditions, see McKusick, 1966.

in which genetic factors are unproved (Table 4). On the whole, the single-gene disorders are extremely rare compared to those of multiple causation, which constitute the major burden of disease in developed countries.[2] In Table 4 we have attempted to include only confirmed

---

[2]For references on individual conditions listed in Table 3, see McKusick, 1966; for references on some of the multifactorial disorders, Table 4, see Damon, 1962, and the sources cited in this paper.

associations, omitting curiosities and single reports, however intriguing (e.g., Kudo, 1968).

DISCUSSION

What use can we make of the clear associations between racial or ethnic group and disease presented so far? The practical scientist can, as mentioned, apply them immediately to the detection, diagnosis, and treatment of disease. A given expenditure of resources will find, cure, and prevent more cervical cancer, syphilis, and tuberculosis among nonwhites in the United States than among whites, for example. In clinical medicine, fever, abdominal pain, and leucocytosis may have different implications in a Northern European (a "surgical" condition like appendicitis or cholecystitis), a Mediterranean (favism, *glucose-6-phosphate dehydrogenase deficiency*, or familial Mediterranean fever), and a Negro (possible sickling crisis). In the two last cases, the patient may be spared needless surgical exploration if the physician is aware of the ethnic and racial associations of disease.

Much more difficult is explaining the associations. Toward this end, we shall follow the useful checklist of MacMahon et al. (1960):

1. Errors of measurement.
2. Differences between groups with respect to more directly associated demographic variables.
3. Differences in environment.
4. Differences in bodily constitution.
5. Differences in genetic constitution.

Errors of Measurement

This first item means that racial or ethnic distributions of disease are liable to distortion due to adequate diagnosis, differential access to and utilization of medical facilities, and lack of precision in estimating populations at risk. Transient residence and low utilization of medical facilities, even within the same medical care plans, are more common among nonwhites than among whites in the United States. Jews, on the other hand, make maximum use of medical facilities in comparison with other white subgroups. As for diagnosis, skin rashes or skin cancer might be harder to diagnose among nonwhites than among whites. Not only have such errors been considered before entering the diseases in Tables 3 and 4, but the internal evidence of the tables—one or another group higher for some diseases, lower for others—shows that no such simple explanation can account for the associations observed.

Differences Between Groups with Respect to More Directly Associated Variables

Some reported differences between groups may reflect differences in age, sex, or socioeconomic status rather than differential disease susceptibility. When disease rates are compared for whites and nonwhites of similar age, sex, and socioeconomic status—in respect to occupation,

Table 4.   *Racial and ethnic disease:multifactorial disorders with a complex or unproved genetic component.*

Ethnic group	High frequency	Low frequency
Ashkenazic Jews	Buerger's disease	Alcoholism
	Diabetes mellitus	Cervical cancer
	Hypercholesterolemia	Pyloric stenosis
	Hyperuricemia	Tuberculosis
	Kaposi's sarcoma	
	Leukemia	
	Pemphigus vulgaris	
	Polycythemia vera	
	Ulcerative colitis and regional enteritis	
Sephardic Jews	Cystic disease of lung	
Northern Europeans	Pernicious anemia	
Irish	Major CNS malformations (anencephaly, encephalocele)	
Chinese	Nasopharyngeal cancer	Chronic lymphatic leukemia
	Trophoblastic disease	Prostatic cancer
Japanese	Cerbrovascular accidents	Acne vulgaris
	Cleft lip-palate	Breast cancer
	Gastric cancer	Chronic lymphatic leukemia
	Trophoblastic disease	Congenital hip disease
		Otosclerosis
		Prostatic cancer
Filipinos (U.S. only)	Hyperuricemia	

Table 4. *Continued*

Ethnic group	High frequency	Low frequency
Polynesians (Hawaiians)	Clubfoot Coronary heart disease Diabetes mellitus	

Africans	Ainhum
	Cervical cancer
	Esophageal cancer
	Hypertension
	Polydactyly
	Prehelical fissure
	Sarcoidosis
	Systemic lupus
	    erythematosus
	Tuberculosis
	Uterine fibroids
		Arteriosclerosis
		Congenital hip disease
		Gallstones
		Major CNS
		    malfunctions
		    (anencephaly,
		    encephalocele)
		Multiple sclerosis
		Osteoporosis and
		    fracture of hip
		    and spine
		Otosclerosis
		Pediculosis capitis
		Polycythemia vera
		Psoriasis
		Pyloric stenosis
		Skin cancer

American Indian	Congenital dislocation of hip Gallbladder disease Rheumatoid arthritis Tuberculosis	Duodenal ulcer
Icelanders	Glaucoma	
Eskimos	Otitis, deafness Salivary gland tumors	

Source. Enlarged from Damon, 1962, and McKusick, 1967.

residence, education, income and the like—and when the differences persist, they cannot be attributed to these demographic variables. Such is the case for many of the disorders in Tables 3 and 4.

Differences in Environment

Apart from the demographic variables associated with socioeconomic status just mentioned, there are many finer differences in customs and way of life. Dietary habits, use of tobacco and alcohol, amount of physical exertion, age at first intercourse or at marriage, number of children, contraceptive and infant-feeding practices differ from one group to another and doubtless underlie many ethnic differences in disease.

The relative contributions of heredity and environment to such differences can be assessed epidemiologically in two ways: by studying disease rates among migrants—that is, the same breeding group in different environments—and among members of different racial or ethnic groups in the "same" environment. (The quotation marks indicate that the micro-environment of an ethnic group need not be identical to that of its neighbor in the same geographic or macro-environment.) For example, rates of stomach cancer are higher for Japanese living in the United States than for American whites. But rates for Japanese living in Hawaii exceed those for Japanese in the mainland United States, while rates for Japanese living in Japan are highest of all. Among the Japanese living in Hawaii, rates of stomach cancer are higher for those born in Japan than for those born in Hawaii. A similar situation holds for nasopharyngeal cancer among Chinese in California. Thus, the causal factors must be associated with a way of life that changes with migration, whether or not a minor genetic factor may also be involved.

On the other hand, Negroes of West African origin have higher blood pressure and more hypertensive disease than whites in a variety of environments in the Caribbean, Panama, and the United States (summarized by Phillips and Burch, 1960; Florey and Cuadrado, 1968). This consistency in various environments argues for heredity.

An example of the comparison of different breeding populations in the "same" environment would be the Hawaiian studies of coronary heart disease already cited (Mollering and Bassett, 1967), showing marked differences among men of pure Hawaiian, part Hawaiian, and Japanese descent. Unfortunately, one cannot be sure how similar their living habits were.

Differences in Body Constitution

This topic brings us closer to the biological associations of interest to the anthropologist and geneticist. A few examples must suffice. *Melanin* protects against sunlight, accounting for the much lower rates of skin cancer among pigmented groups. The Negro *ectoderm* responds to injury with excessive connective tissue to form keloids, or raised scars. Connective tissue from Caucasians, Negroes, Eskimos, and American Indians is reported to differ in amount and composition (Boucek et al., 1958).

The increased density of Negro bone (Trotter, Broman, and Peterson, 1960) may in part account for the relatively low frequency of spine and hip fractures among elderly Negroes (Bollet et al., 1965; Moldawer et al., 1965). On the other hand, despite the reduced bone density of Orientals, presumed to be genetic (Garn et al., 1964), Wong (1965) reported lower rates of forearm fractures among Chinese and Malays in Singapore than among Swedes in Sweden. Negroes have markedly lower frequencies of Legg-Perthes disease, an osteochondrosis of the femoral head affecting mainly young males, than do Caucasians. However, American Indians, who may also have lower frequencies of Legg-Perthes disease, are much more susceptible to congenital dislocation of the hip than whites, whereas Negroes are markedly less so. Anatomical differences in the shape of the *acetabulum* have been adduced in explanation.

The nasal index, breadth/length, varies with humidity and inversely with latitude (Weiner, 1964). The long, narrow nose of Eskimos is not wholly successful as an adaptation to a cold, dry environment. This may explain in part their frequent upper respiratory infections, leading to draining ears and deafness (Brody and McAlister, 1965), in contrast to Africans and Malayans.

The rarity of pediculosis capitis (head lice) among Negroes is unexplained but may relate to some characteristic of the scalp or hair.

A physiological characteristic that varies among breeding populations is the level of immunity against micro-organisms. Lacking previous exposure, some groups are extremely susceptible to diseases that are mild in other populations. Fatal epidemics of measles and upper respiratory infections among Eskimos and Melanesians, smallpox among American Indians, and susceptibility to tuberculosis among all of these groups as well as Negroes, have been well documented. On the other hand, Ashkenazic Jews are relatively resistant to tuberculosis, presumably because they have lived for centuries under crowded conditions where only the resistant survived. Negroes appear relatively resistant to vivax malaria, for similar selective reasons (Bruce-Chwatt, 1967).

Research into the disease and immunological status of the few remaining isolates, unexposed to the larger culture, can contribute greatly to our understanding of disease as a selective factor in evolution, the history and geography of disease, and our knowledge of human origins and distribution (Hackett, 1963; Hudson, 1963, 1965; World Health Organization, 1968).

One way to demonstrate the reality of racial differences in physiological and biochemical functions, some of which underlie differences in disease frequency and severity, is by a list, as in Table 5. Further research will undoubtedly disclose many more racial differences than appear in this partial list. Race is clearly more than skin deep. In fact, the validity of the classical scheme of human races, described morpho-

Table 5. *Some racial differences in physiological and biochemical norms.*

Trait	In relation to Caucasoids[a]	
	Negroids	Mongoloids
Birth		
Weight	−	−
Skeletal maturation	+	
Dental maturation	+	
Neurological maturation	+	
Neonatal motor development	+	
Acuity, auditory and visual	+	
Blood pressure	+	−
Bone density	+	−
Color blindness	−	−
Corneal arcus	+	
Fibrinolysin activity	+	
Isoniazid inactivation		+
Keloid formation	+	
Lactase deficiency (adult)	+	+
Pulmonary function	−	
Serum globulins	+	
Skin resistance, electrical	+	
Tasting, phenylthiocarbamide	+	+
Twinning, dizygotic	+	−

[a]Plus sign indicates "greater than"; minus sign indicates "less than."

logically by early anthropologists and subsequently confirmed on serological grounds, is independently substantiated by physiological and pathological evidence. Some of the three-way distributions, as for bone density, twinning, and possibly blood pressure, are particularly striking.

Differences in Genetic Constitution

Such differences determine many of the bodily characteristics just mentioned, such as skin color or bone density. For only a few of the single-gene disorders in Table 3 is there evidence for *heterozygote* advantage, the mechanism usually postulated for the persistence of such deleterious genes in numbers beyond those expected from mutation—that is, as "*balanced polymorphisms.*" Hemoglobin S has been shown to confer resistance to falciparum malaria in heterozygotes. The same is strongly suspected but not yet fully established for other abnormal *hemoglobins,* for glucose-6-phosphate dehydrogenase deficiency, and for *thalassemia.* Increased fertility, another aspect of heterozygote advantage besides resistance to disease, has been reported for carriers of cystic fibrosis (Knudson, Wayne, and Hallett, 1967), and suggested, together with improved survival, for heterozygote carriers of Tay-Sachs disease (Myrianthopoulos and Aronson, 1966).

But with almost 30% of human genetic loci estimated to be polymorphic, and with most of these probably "relics" of previous selective crises (Bodmer, 1968), we have a long way to go in accounting for them all and probably never can.

The genetic component is overwhelming in the single-gene disorders. In the multicausal disorders, environmental factors tend to dominate the genetic ones. There is little doubt, for example, that alcoholism, tuberculosis, and cervical cancer are largely environmental in origin. But even for tuberculosis, an infectious disease most common in low-income, crowded communities, several twin studies—for example, Harvald and Hauge (1965)—have shown a genetic substrate, and the disease is much more frequent and severe among Negroes than among white persons, independent of childhood infection (Lurie, 1964). Incidentally, it should be noted that diseases with a genetic component need not be associated with race—for example, peptic ulcer (Damon and Polednak, 1967).

Diseases which change in frequency or manifestations over periods too short for genetic influences (*mutation, selection,* gene flow, *drift*) to operate must be mainly environmental in origin. Examples relevant here are the decline in mortality from hypertension and cervical cancer, and the oscillations in leukemia rates in the United States during the last thirty to forty years.

In connection with the genetic influences just noted, McKusick (1967) points out that no racial or ethnic differences in mutation rates have been found and that gene flow as well as mutation could account for the occasional occurrence of, say, cystic fibrosis in an American Negro.

A further difficulty in assessing the genetic component in the multifactorial diseases in Table 4 is that the genetic component is *polygenic* rather than *monogenic,* as in the simply inherited disorders of Table 3. Variability in both the genetic and the environmental determinants of disease means that one cannot expect associations to hold or to be equally strong among all populations at all times or in the same population at different times and in different places. Research among racially mixed populations, as well as among the isolates, the migrants, and the different sedentary groups living in the same environment already discussed, should help settle these questions.

SUMMARY

Differences in disease as well as in physiological and biochemical function have been documented among the major classical races of man, as well as among a variety of breeding populations which are ethnically or culturally as well as biologically distinct. The diseases and the functional characteristics of racial or ethnic groups are both monogenic and polygenic; polygenic diseases often have a strong environmental component as well.

Some of the most striking associations are the virtually exclusive concentration of certain single-gene disorders in one or another group, such as *pentosuria, dysautonomia*, and the *lipoidoses* among Jews, thalassemia and familial Mediterranean fever among Mediterranean peoples, and sickle-cell and some other *hemoglobinopathies* among Africans. Of the multifactorial diseases of complex or uncertain inheritance, there is a relatively high frequency of diabetes, leukemia, polycythemia vera, and ulcerative colitis among Jews, hypertension, *polydactyly,* and *sarcoidosis* among Negroes, and diabetes and coronary heart disease among Polynesians (Hawaiians). Twinning frequency, bone density, lactase deficiency, and auditory and visual acuity also differ among the major races of man.

Distinctive racial or ethnic patterns of disease can be profitably applied by the public health official to the detection and prevention of disease and by the clinician in diagnosis and treatment. The anthropologist can gain insight into human origins, relationships, distribution, and adaptation. The geneticist has new material for the study of heredity in human populations. And finally the epidemiologist gains clues to the cause of some of man's major diseases, with the ultimate hope of eradication.

REFERENCES

Bodmer, W. F. 1968. Demographic approaches to the measurement of differential selection in human populations. *Proc. Nat. Acad. Sci.* 59: 690–699.

Bollett, A. J., G. Engh, and W. Parson. 1965. Epidemiology of osteoporasis. *Arch. Int. Med* 116: 191–194.

Boucek, R. J., N. L. Noble, K. T. Kao, and H. R. Elden. 1958. The effects of age, sex, and race upon the acetic acid fractions of collagen (human biopsy-connective tissue). *J. Gerontol.* 13: 2–9.

Brody, J. A., and R. McAlister, 1965. Draining ears and deafness among Alaskan Eskimos. *Arch Otolaryngol.* 81: 29–33.

Bruce-Chwatt, L. J. 1967. Malaria. In P. B. Beeson and W. McDermott, eds., *Textbook of medicine.* Philadelphia: Saunders.

Damon, A. 1962. Some host factors in disease: Sex, race, ethnic group, and body form. *J. Nat. Med. Assoc.* 54: 424–431.

Damon, A., and A. P. Polednak. 1967. Constitution, genetics, and body form in peptic ulcer: A review. *J. Chronic Dis.* 20: 787–802.

Florey, C. Du V., and R. R. Cuadrado. 1968. Blood pressure in native Cape Verdeans and in Cape Verdean immigrants and their descendants living in New England. *Hum. Biol.* 40: 189–211.

Garn, S. M. 1965. *Human races.* 2d ed. Springfield, Illinois: Charles C Thomas.

Garn, S. M., E. M. Pao, and M. E. Rihl, 1964. Compact bone in Chinese and Japanese. *Science* 143: 1439–1440.

Hackett, C. J. 1963. On the origin of the human treponematoses. *Bull. World Health. Org.* 29: 7–41.

Harvald, B., and H. M. Hauge. 1965. Hereditary factors elucidated by twin studies. In J. V. Neel et al., eds., *Genetics and the epidemiology of chronic diseases.* U.S. Public Health Service, Publication No. 1163. Washington, D.C.: Government Printing Office.

Hudson, E. H. 1963. Treponematosis and anthropology. *Ann. Int. Med.* 58: 1037–1048.

Hudson, E. H. 1965. Treponematosis and man's social evolution. *Amer. Anthrop.* 67: 885–901.

Knudson, A. G., L. Wayne, and W. Y. Hallett. 1967. On the selective advantage of cystic fibrosis heterozygotes. *Amer. J. Hum. Genet.* 19: 388–392.

Kudo, T. 1968. Spontaneous occlusion of the circle of Willis. A disease apparently confined to Japanese. *Neurology* 18: 485–496.

Lurie, M. B. 1964. *Resistance to tuberculosis.* Cambridge, Mass.: Harvard Univ. Press.

McKusick, V. A. 1966. *Mendelian inheritance in man.* Catalogue of autosomal dominant, autosomal recessive, and X-linked phenotypes. Baltimore: Johns Hopkins Press.

McKusick, V. A. 1967. The ethnic distribution of disease in the United States. *J. Chronic Dis.* 20: 115–118.

MacMahon, B., T. F. Pugh, and J. Ibsen. 1960. *Epidemiologic methods.* Boston: Little, Brown.

Moellering, R. C., and D. R. Bassett. 1967. Myocardial infarction in Hawaiian and Japanese males on Oahu—a review of 505 cases occurring between 1955 and 1964. *J. Chronic Dis.* 20: 89–101.

Moldawer, M., S. J. Zimmerman, and L. C. Collins. 1965. Incidence of osteoporosis in elderly whites and elderly Negroes. *J. Amer. Med. Assoc.* 194: 85–862.

Myrianthopoulos, N. C., and S. M. Aronson. 1966. Population dynamics of Tay-Sachs disease, I. Reproductive fitness and selection. *Amer. J. Hum. Genet.* 18: 313–327.

Phillips, J. H., and G. E. Burch. 1960. A review of cardiovascular diseases in the white and Negro races. *Medicine* 39: 241–288.

Shimkin, M. B., and D. B. Loveland. 1961. A note on mortality from lymphatic leukemia in Oriental populations in the United States. *Blood* 17: 736–766.

Sievers, M. L., and J. R. Marquis. 1962. Duodenal ulcer among Southwestern American Indians. *Gastroenterology* 42: 566–569.

Sloan, N. R. 1963. Ethnic distribution of diabetes mellitus in Hawaii. *J. Amer. Med Assoc.* 183: 419–424.

Smith, R. L. 1956a. Recorded and expected mortality among the Japanese of the United States and Hawaii, with special reference to cancer. *J. Nat. Cancer Inst.* 17: 459–473.

Smith, R. L. 1956b. Recorded and expected mortality among the Chinese of Hawaii and the United States, with special reference to cancer. *J. Nat. Cancer Inst.* 17:667-676.

Trotter, M., G. E. Broman, and R. R. Peterson. 1960. Densities of bones of white and Negro skeletons. *J. Bone Jt. Surg.* 42-A: 50–58.

Wagner, C. J., and E. S. Rabeau. 1964. Indian poverty and Indian health. *Health, Education, and Welfare Indicators,* March, pp. 24–44.

Weiner, J. S. 1964. Climatic adaptation. In G. A. Harrison, J. S. Weiner, J. M. Tanner, and N. A. Barnicot, *Human biology.* New York: Oxford Univ. Press.

Wong, P. C. N. 1965. Epidemiology of fractures of the forearm among the major racial groups in Singapore. *Acta Orthop. Scand.* 36: 168–178.

World Health Organization. 1968. *Research on human population genetics.* Tech. Rept. 387. Geneva, Switzerland.

Social Factors

The human population has changed through time and will continue to do so. This is also true for its component parts, the so-called races. The physical variability of different groups and their constant change through time has existed as far back as man's record can be traced. Equally ancient is man's possession of culture. In fact, culture is older than our species; it is even older than our genus. It has constituted the prime adaptation of all forms of mankind to the terrestrial environment for nearly two million years. Viewed across this time span, the improvement in the capacity for culture has been the most outstanding characteristic of human evolution.

Social Behavior and Human Diversity

FREDERICK S. HULSE
Department of Anthropology
University of Arizona
Tucson, Arizona

Races are temporary phenomena, evolutionary episodes, always subject to change and always destined to vanish. For a long time, scholars have attempted to classify human races in the same manner that the *species*[1] and genera of animals are classified. The more we have learned about human biology, the less possible and less reasonable such attempts have appeared. A species is a closed unit genetically, whereas a race is not. Consequently, a species is "pure," whereas all races are now and always have been "impure," that is, with genes derived from various other races. The human species *Homo sapiens* forms a genetic continuum and gene flow is open between its constituent populations.

Our species has changed through time by means of *evolution*. An earlier form, *Homo erectus*, became *Homo sapiens*, which eventually may evolve into still another species or may instead become extinct. These two ways of vanishing are also open to any race, of course, but a race is far more likely to disappear by merging, through intermixture, with other races.

---

[1]Words defined in the Glossary (p. 173) are italicized the first time they appear in each paper.

In contrast to other human groupings, a race may remain in existence for a long time; the earliest fossil remains of humans from North America are essentially indistinguishable from the skeletons of modern American Indians living one thousand generations later. But from an evolutionary viewpoint, one thousand generations is a very short time. Our species, *sapiens*, has been in existence at least three times as long, and our genus, *Homo*, at least thirty times as long.

Human populations had already inhabited almost all of the Old World more than half a million years ago, during the mid-Pleistocene epoch. Fossil remains of ancestral humans assigned by modern taxonomists to the species *Homo erectus* have been found as far apart as western Europe, eastern Asia, Java, northern and central Africa, and possibly even southern Africa. Tools made by such people have been found in all of these regions and in most of the intermediate areas as well. There can be little doubt that these populations were as similar to one another in those days as the populations inhabiting the same regions are today. All the lower jawbones are heavy, nearly chinless, with teeth that are clearly human rather than apish. All the skulls are thick, with large brow ridges and low foreheads. Cranial capacity was much greater than that of any ape, although not up to modern standards. Perfectly erect posture had been attained even earlier than the mid-Pleistocene epoch, and the evidence of the tools attests to manipulative skill as great as our own and a mentality superior to that of any other animal.

Differences in anatomical detail between fossil remains from different parts of the world have been noted. For instance, the mid-Pleistocene Javanese may have been taller than the Chinese and certainly had smaller brains. The Heidelberg jaw discovered near Mauer, Germany, is exceptionally large, though the teeth are within the modern range. The skull cap from Olduvai Gorge in East Africa has by far the largest brow ridges. Weidenreich (1943) has noted more than a dozen traits shared by Sinanthropus of the mid-Pleistocene in northern China with modern Mongoloids rather than with all modern peoples. The ascending bones of the jaw from Ternifine in northern Africa slope backward, as those from other places do not.

Some differences of technology must be noted, too. The Ternifine tools are from a tool-making tradition very different from that of Sinanthropus. Only with Sinanthropus do we have evidence of the control of fire, and indeed cooking. Perhaps Europeans and Africans lacked this convenience for some hundreds of thousands of years after Orientals acquired it. The evidence is too scanty for us to be certain of anything except that our ancestors had spread to vast areas and showed signs of both biological and cultural variation by the early part of the second, or Mindel-Riss, interglacial period, perhaps half a million years ago.

Since that time between twenty and thirty thousand human generations have elapsed, and our species has spread to still other parts of the world. Arctic tundras, tropical islets, deserts, high plateaus, and equatorial rain forests have been occupied. These areas present diverse hazards to man's existence. The presence or absence of intense cold, scanty natural food supplies, reduced oxygen pressure at high altitudes, heavy humidity, continued heat, insect and water-borne infections are just a few among many ways in which the natural environment varies from one region to another.

When any species extends its habitat, some of its local populations are bound to be subjected to new sorts of stresses. The greater the extent of the habitat, the greater will be the variety of conditions to which these populations must adapt. Traits that are useless or even harmful in one area may be advantageous in another. Consequently, *genes* and combinations of genes at different *loci* that are subject to negative *selection* in one locality are often subject to positive selection in another part of the range. At the same time, most mating is likely to take place among creatures inhabiting the same area, if only because it is easier. Among creatures living in social bands, as most primates do, each social group may easily become a separate *gene pool* (Washburn and Devore, 1961). In combination, these factors tend to promote diversification based upon locality within any species. The earliest fossil representatives of *Homo sapiens* show distinct signs of local differentiation wherever we find them.

Given such conditions, one might have expected that several different species of mankind would have evolved, just as several species of baboon have done in a far more restricted part of the world. Yet this has not occurred. Indeed, there is no reason to believe that such a process ever began. Men and women from all parts of the world have mated and produced offspring showing no sign whatever of reduced genetic efficiency. No two human breeding populations differ enough genetically to be considered incipient species. Clearly there have been natural forces at work to maintain the unity of the human stock, and these forces have been strong enough to hold in check any tendencies to purely local *adaptations*.

The plasticity of the human *phenotype* is certainly one of the factors concerned. Our bodies can adjust to a great range of conditions. We are able to live, work, and reproduce even when fed much less than we would like to eat. Protective *antibodies* are formed in our blood streams when foreign proteins invade us. At high altitudes, we soon begin to produce more red blood cells. We become acclimatized to frigid as well as to torrid weather. Our musculature develops, at least during youth, if we get enough exercise. Our minds, too, are plastic and flexible. Youngsters learn English as easily as they do Chinese or Choctaw. They are capable of developing the most diverse preferences, prejudices, and perceptions, all in accordance with the social groups within which they are raised and trained. Oddly enough, even when fully adult, humans can learn new things and change their values, at least to some degree. We are highly educable, and this is an important aspect of our plasticity.

Indeed, educability is probably the most vital aspect of human plasticity, for it is intimately concerned with the development of human culture, and human culture is our true *ecological* niche. All animal species must adapt to climate, to food supply, to disease. Animals that live in socially organized groups, like wolves or baboons for instance, must adapt to their society as well. We are by no means unique among animal species in the ability to respond flexibly, but we are unique in the extent to which this ability is expressed. Our ancestors, a long time ago, began to develop culture, and having done so they had to adapt to the new ways of life made possible by culture. This has been a universal characteristic of mankind for as far back in time as the record shows, and it has had a unifying effect upon human evolution.

The earliest evidence of cultural activities actually long antedates the earliest fossil evidence of the genus *Homo*. Pebble tools—crude and simple, to be sure, but clearly prepared intentially for use—have been found in close association with "Zinjanthropus," an Australopithecine (a primate of an extinct genus) who lived nearly two million years ago in East Africa. Since that time, technology has modified the physical environment of man to a greater and greater extent, and it is to the technologically modified environment that we have had to adapt. Both hand and brain have been subjected to new demands. Dexterity in manipulation, ability to imitate the tool-making techniques of other persons, and even more, ability to conceive of new tool types and new uses for tools have had a selective value among humans from that day to this. Within any band or troop of protohominids, individuals deficient in these abilities would certainly have had fewer chances to reproduce and rear their offspring successfully. In competition between bands, the use of tools in exploiting natural resources must have given a solid advantage to the bands that were more expert.

It is interesting to note in this connection that among all peoples today the use of the right hand in skilled operations is culturally preferred and is probably inherited. It is also interesting that as tools improved, teeth and jaws became smaller and the degree of prognathism (forward projection of the jaws) decreased. The mouth had less hard work to do, and the selective value of strong jaw muscles declined. Consequently, the buttressing of heavy brow ridges ceased to be necessary. Early closure of the cranial sutures, which is useful if a young creature needs strong jaw muscles, was no longer advantageous. Another year or two of rapid brain growth for the child turned out to be a better investment for the species, and such continued brain growth is inconsistent with early suture closing.

Furthermore, manufacturing and using tools made it possible for our ancestors to shift from a vegetarian to a largely carnivorous diet in all parts of the world, and this change of dietary habit necessitated changes in social habit too. Nonhuman primates do not share their food, but animals hunting in packs, such as wolves, are likely to do so; food will be brought home to the young at least. If the young grow slowly and demand much care from their mothers, as they do among primates, the latter will be less able to hunt than are the males. Bands in which the males bring meat home to be shared are bound to have a selective advantage over those in which the males neglect to do so. This activity demands psychological characteristics that people in all societies possess, and which are lacking among other primates. The sexual division of labor, like right-handedness and tool-manufacture, is one of the universals of culture.

The fossil record cannot give us direct information on most aspects of nonmaterial culture, but we can make a number of very reasonable estimates if we study that record closely. Language is one of the most vital of the nonmaterial aspects of culture and is a cultural universal. Indeed, some scholars deny that culture could exist without language. There can be no doubt that this faculty confers an enormous selective advantage. In early times any band of hominids that had learned to speak would certainly have been far more successful in any of their endeavors than a band that had not. Once it came into existence, language must have spread very rapidly throughout the entire species. When did it come into existence?

Sinanthropus, you will recall, controlled fire by the mid-Pleistocene, half a million years ago—a complicated procedure. According to Wallace (1961), it involves keeping a fire going for indefinite periods, which cannot be done without a fuel supply; forethought as well as cleverness is required. It involves keeping the fire where it belongs, where it will be useful rather than dangerous; judgment and constant attention are required. It involves being able to transport or kindle fire, both of which require patience and self-control. It involves a way of life in which fire is a useful tool, for warmth, cooking, illumination, preparing other tools, and other purposes—a way of life rather unlike that of any other animal.

Could such a complex social existence be maintained if the members of the group could not talk to one another? I feel uncertain, but it makes me wonder.

Furthermore, at least one of the individuals whose fossil remains have been found at the Sinanthropus site in northern China appears to be a female past the age of child bearing. The survival of the elderly is rarely observed among wild animals; the old have no function. In all human societies, however, they may babysit, make or repair artifacts, and pass on vital information to the younger, more active generation. Their accumulated knowledge benefits the society to which they belong—if they can talk. Genes for longevity must have begun to possess added survival value after language began to be used. Among present-day populations there seem to be no genetic differences in potential longevity, although, of course, the chance of early death is much greater in societies lacking adequate nutrition and sanitation. Human culture has certainly led to the same sort of selection pressure throughout the entire species—pressure in favor of such previously disadvantageous traits as delay in maturity and a prolonged life span. It may have started as long ago as the time of Sinanthropus.

Even if we doubt the existence of such cultural traits as language and care of the feeble as long ago as the second interglacial period, some half million years ago, it is difficult to deny their presence by the end of the third, among the Neanderthaloids. Fossil remains like those of the cripple at Shanidar in the Near East described by Steward (1959) give us proof of such care, and excavated graves often accompanied by grave goods indicate that they also had language. These people must have had ideas about death, which they shared with one another. The only way in which ideas can be shared is through language. Emotions may be communicated from creature to creature without words. Instructions may be given and understood by means of gestures and example. But rituals like those involved in the disposal of the dead imply that beliefs and ethical judgments had begun to affect or indeed to govern some aspects of human behavior.

Communication of beliefs through language has often influenced man genetically. The incest taboo, for instance, is characteristic of all known societies today. The definition of incest varies; one may be forbidden to mate with anyone of the same clan, or perhaps with a sister-in-law or the child of a godfather, as well as with one's parents and siblings. But one is always denied sexual access to persons who are linguistically classified as certain sorts of close kinfolk. The result of these rules, whatever their details, is to reduce the extent of closely *consanguineous* matings. Among humans the incest taboo has acted as a strong force to keep the lines of genetic communication open between adjacent groups, and gene flow has therefore been much greater, more constant, and a stronger unifying force than among other primates. Mating between adjacent groups and bands has been promoted, offering a far better opportunity for forming new genetic combinations and increasing *heterozygosity*. Even more important, it has provided for the spread of new mutations from their point of origin to other populations.

In all historic and late prehistoric times, intentional and widespread migration has also served as a force to keep the human species unified. Here again culture has influenced the direction of human evolution, for migration has become easier as technology has improved. After the expansion of *Homo erectus* throughout the Old World, we do not know how much wandering back and forth took place. The persistent difference in tool styles between eastern Asia and the rest of the Old World suggests a minimum of population movements between these areas, although gene flow presumably was constant. The spread of changes in tool styles from the Mediterranean area into Africa, however, suggests that migration did take place between these two regions. Archaeological evidence suggests extensive migrations by the Upper Palaeolithic—perhaps 30,000 years ago—and indicates more and more tribal movements in each succeeding period.

Culture has so modified the way of life of our species that *orthoselection* to improve the capacity for culture has been the most outstanding characteristic of human evolution. However, while culture has tended to equalize the circumstances of man's life—for the requirements of human life have been the same in all places and during all periods—no matter where man lives, nature has tended to make those circumstances differ. As with other animals, the major factor accounting for differences in *allele* frequencies between different populations is geography. Each population has had to adapt to purely local hazards. In some areas, *endemic* malaria has led to increased frequency of one or another abnormal *hemoglobin* (Livingston, 1967). In others, low oxygen pressure has led to an enlarged lung capacity and an increased supply of hemoglobin (Hurtado, 1932). In the desert it is adaptive to have a spare body build and in a cloudy area to have skin light enough to absorb ultraviolet rays (Garn, 1961).

It is necessary at this point to note that the particular cultures of peoples living in various regions also have influenced the ways in which adaptation has taken place. The clearings that Africans made in order to practice agriculture permitted malaria-transmitting mosquitoes to breed more readily. Dependence upon one-crop agriculture was likely to lead to protein deficiency and in turn to dysentery (Scrimshaw, Tay-

lor and Gordon, 1959), which acted as a selective force. Population
increase, due to food production, has often led to more rapid spread of
contagious disease and the eventual selection of mutations that provide immunity from one disease or another. Only such cultural devices
as warm clothing and excellent hunting techniques permitted populations to occupy Arctic areas where the climate then acted as a selection
force to promote the survival and thus the reproduction of those individuals with biological traits best suited to withstanding intense cold. As
cultures have changed over the millenia, the adaptations of various
peoples have changed too, making the reconstruction of racial history
a dubious undertaking, even when there is a great deal of *osteological
data*.

While culture in general has been a unifying influence in the evolution of the human species, particular cultures have often tended to act
as divisive forces. Religious, linguistic, economic, and occupational
barriers to gene flow are among the creations of the human mind, and
they are more difficult to surmount than mountains, deserts, or oceans.
The fact that caste *endogamy* is practiced in such countries as India
and the United States has led to the existence of separate breeding
populations which, although living side by side, retain quite different
gene frequencies at various loci (Workman et al., 1963; Olivier, 1961).

The configuration of gene frequencies in any population may influence
the growth pattern, resistance to disease, age changes during senility,
and the biochemistry of body fluids just as it may influence details of
facial appearance or bodily proportions. Races are *not* assemblages of
individuals who simply resemble one another in some visible way. There
is no race of albinos, despite the fact that albinism is genetically determined. Some Hopi are albinos, as are some Swedes and Nigerians,
although all three belong to different races. But the Hopi tend to mate
with one another rather than with Swedes and Nigerians who also tend
to mate within their own groups, and these populations—not individuals
assembled together because they share a certain trait—are what may
be called races.

It should also be noted that such racial differences have nothing to
do with the mental or anatomical requirements for full participation
in culture. As an expression of goodwill toward groups whose members
differ in appearance from us, some people have said that racial differences are only skin deep. While only metaphorical, this statement is
somewhat misleading. It is much more accurate, though less dramatic,
to say that racial differences are irrelevant to the problems of adjusting
to any one particular culture. Racial differences in physiological adapta-

tion among living populations are marked, but this does not make them relevant to psychic function.

It is just as misleading to think of races only in terms of constant redivisions in human stocks when rejoinings are just as constant. Since the voyages of Columbus, populations of the world have been redistributed on a grand scale. New mixtures of all sorts have taken place so that the present-day genetic distinctions between the inhabitants of different parts of the world are constantly being reduced, and at the same time new races are being brought into existence. Racial variety has been and still is biologically useful to the human species.

REFERENCES

Garn, S. M. 1961. *Human races.* Springfield, Ill.: Charles C Thomas.

Hurtado, A. 1932. Respiratory adaptation in the Indians native to the Peruvian Andes. *Amer. J. Phys. Anthrop.* 17: 137–165.

Livingstone, F. B. 1967. *Abnormal hemoglobins in human populations.* Chicago: Aldine Press.

Olivier, G. 1961 *Anthropologie des Tamouls du Sud de L'Inde.* Paris: Masson.

Scrimshaw, N. S., C. E. Taylor, and J. E. Gordon. 1959. Interaction of nutrition and infection. *Amer. J. Med. Sci.* 237: 367–403.

Stewart, T. D. 1959. The restored Shanidar I skull. *Smithsonian Report for 1958.* Smithsonian Institution, Washington, D.C. Pp. 473–480.

Wallace, A. F. C. 1961. *Culture and personality.* New York: Random House.

Washburn, S. L., and I. Devore. 1961. Social behavior of baboons and early man. In *Social life of early man.* Viking Fund Publications in Anthropology, No. 1, New York.

Weidenreich, F. 1943. The skull of Sinanthropus Pekinensis. *Palaeontologica Sinica, New Series D,* No. 10, Pekin.

Workman, P. L., B. S. Blumberg, and A. J. Cooper. 1963. Selection, gene migration, and polymorphic stability in a U. W. white and Negro population. *Amer. J. Hum. Genet.* 15: 429–437.

Improperly compiled statistics, prejudicially interpreted, have provided a formidable base for many misconceptions concerning race, mental illness, and intelligence. Most certainly differences exist between the races, the inescapable consequence of the kinds of social and environmental factors that correlate with race in our complex society and which serve to hinder individuals from reaching their maximum inherited potential for both intelligence and mental health. All indications are that racial-group I.Q. scores would be equalized in the absence of social and environmental inequities. The real challenge is to provide an environment in which members of all racial groups can reach their maximum capabilities, to the benefit of the entire society as well as themselves. In this respect it should be noted that even with the present forms of I.Q. testing, the range of individual differences within each racial group far exceeds the differences cited as existing between the groups.

Race, Mental Illness and Intelligence: A Social Psychological View

THOMAS F. PETTIGREW
Department of Social Relations
Harvard University
Cambridge, Massachusetts

The 1840 Census of the United States proved to be a bombshell. In the midst of the brewing storm over slavery, this census presented truly amazing data on mental illness and intelligence among Negro Americans (Litwack, 1961; Stanton, 1960). Though there were no appreciable regional differences for whites, the reported ratio for "insane" and "idiotic" Negroes was only one in every 1,558 in the South, but one in every 144.5 in the North.[1] Even more startling was the near-perfect correlation of

---

This paper is drawn from a fuller statement of these and related topics which appeared in: T. F. Pettigrew, 1964. *A Profile of the Negro American.* Van Nostrand, Princeton, N.J.

[1]Postell's (1953) analysis of the records of pre-Civil War southern estates as recorded in probate courts of the time indicates that the ratio of slaves suffering from mental illness and retardation was roughly one per 86, a figure over 18 times that cited by the 1840 census.

rate with geography. In Maine every fourteenth Negro was recorded either "insane" or "idiotic"; in Massachusetts, one in every 43; in New Jersey, one of every 297; while Virginia had only one in 1,229; and Louisiana had only one in 4,310. Here were the juicy figures into which a pro-slavery fire-eater could sink his teeth. Obviously, slavery was a benign institution, protecting the Negro from the rigors of competitive society that so quickly either drove him mad or reduced him to idiocy. Abolition of slavery, argued John Calhoun immediately, would thus prove to be a "curse instead of a blessing."

Soon a young physician and statistician, Dr. Edward Jarvis of Massachusetts, challenged the accuracy of the census. Finding such glaring errors as Northern communities with more reported "insane" and "idiotic" Negroes than their total Negro populations, Jarvis completely refuted the incredible data. "It was the census that was insane," pithily commented a Northern clergyman, "and not the colored people."

MENTAL ILLNESS

Ever since the census of 1840, the mental illness rates of Negroes have been a subject of considerable interest and debate. But formidable methodological problems must be overcome before any reasonably accurate estimate can be made of the "true" amount of psychosis and neurosis existing in the general population. For many years investigators merely counted the number of people detained at any one time in mental institutions. This procedure is obviously inadequate. Such a rate not only reflects the number of mentally ill persons, but also the duration of confinement, the availability and quality of the treatment facilities, and a host of other factors unrelated to the immediate problem. Consequently, later investigators have employed rates of mental illness over a specified time period. Two distinctly different types of rates exist—"incidence" and "prevalence." Incidence refers to the number of new cases of a disease occurring in a population during a particular time interval, while prevalence refers to the total number of active cases of a disease present in a particular population during a particular time interval. Thus, prevalence includes new cases together with old cases who have either continuously remained ill or have elapsed. This distinction is a vital one, for the two types of rates may lead to diverse conclusions.

Though the use of specified time period and of both incidence and prevalence rates mark definite improvements in technique, serious problems remain. Generally, only the data from public institutions are secured, causing an underestimation of mental illness among those who can afford private treatment. And even studies which carefully include both public and private patients leave uncounted the many mentally ill people who never receive treatment. Equally serious problems are raised by the absence of a rigorous conception of mental illness and the dependence upon psychiatric diagnoses. Various researchers have employed different definitions of mental illness, introducing error that is often compounded by unreliable medical judgments.

Further complications involve the special position and treatment of Negroes in American society. Since Negroes as a group are less educated and less attuned to the mass media than whites, they are less informed about mental disorder. A survey conducted in four Texas communities revealed that the Negro respondents were more likely to believe that the mentally ill "just don't want to face their problems," lack "will power," and look different from other people (Crawford et al., 1960). Such beliefs together with inadequate financial resources to care for the disturbed family members at home often lead to the more rapid institutional commitment of Negroes. In addition, some Southern juries commit Negroes to mental institutions more readily than whites (Friedsam et al., 1954). Once committed, Negro lower-class patients, like lower-class patients in general, are less likely to receive advanced therapy; indeed, they may well receive only custodial care and thus be consigned to lengthy institutionalization (Crawford et al., 1960; Malzberg, 1944; Stewart, 1955). This is especially true in the South, where virtually all private facilities are closed to Negroes, and the few public facilities open to them are symbolic instruments of white-supremacy state governments—segregated, inferior, and grossly overcrowded. These factors operate to elevate spuriously both the incidence and prevalence mental illness rates of Negroes, since they amplify the number of Negroes institutionalized without necessarily representing an actual increase in the amount of mental illness.

Mindful of these sharply limiting qualifications, a few broad generalizations can be tentatively ventured on the basis of available evidence. Consider first the psychoses, the most severe mental aberrations. Repeated studies of first admissions to state hospitals in a variety of areas generally show Negro incidence rates for psychosis to be about twice as high as white rates[2] (Clark, 1949; Frumkin, 1954; Ivins, 1950; Malzberg, 1944, 1953, 1956, 1959; Pasamanick, 1963; Williams and Carmichael, 1949; Wilson and Lantz, 1957). Particular psychoses contribute disproportionately to the greater Negro rates. Schizophrenia, the bizarre condition of social withdrawal and personality disorganization, is especially

---

[2]For methodological criticisms of these studies, see Schermerhorn (1956).

frequent among Negro first admissions. Two organic diagnoses, paresis and alcoholic psychosis, are also over-represented among Negroes entering state hospitals.

But such state hospital research obviously underestimates the amount of white psychosis. Allowances must be made for the fact that whites are better able to afford private treatment and thus escape enumeration in these studies of public facilities. Investigations that attempt to overcome this difficulty by including private facilities have turned up conflicting results. In Pasamanick's (1963) study of prevalence rates in Baltimore, the Negro psychosis rate was roughly twice that of whites for state hospitals alone, but when the predominantly white private and veterans' hospitals were included, the Negro-to-white ratio was lowered to one-and-a-half to one. Jaco's (1960) Texas study of incidence, however, found that the Negro rates were actually below that of "Anglo-Americans" once both private as well as public first admissions were calculated.

Finally, there is the problem of ascertaining how many mentally ill persons remain unhospitalized and untreated. As can be readily imagined, research on this problem is extremely difficult. One preliminary effort, a Baltimore health survey, found that the noninstitutionalized prevalence rate for psychosis was roughly ten times higher for whites than Negroes; but serious methodological weaknesses cast doubt upon this remarkable finding[3] (Pasamanick, 1963).

Obviously, the definitive epidemiological research on this question is yet to be performed. Meanwhile, personality tests confirm a greater tendency among Negroes to report psychotic symptoms. Two investigations independently conducted on diverse populations noted that Negro males scored significantly higher than comparable white males on the Minnesota Multiphasic Inventory (MMPI) scales measuring psychotic trends (Caldwell, 1959; Hokanson and Calden, 1960). Illustrative items from these scales include: "I have had periods in which I carried on activities without knowing later what I had been doing," and "At times I have had fits of laughing and crying that I cannot control." On balance,

---

[3]The weaknesses were threefold: (1) the noninstitutional prevalance rates were projected from just 17 actual cases of psychosis. (2) The problem of reliable and valid diagnoses was particularly acute, for internists, not psychiatrists, examined the subjects and often diagnosed mental disorders without psychiatric consultation or psychometric testing. Subsequently, one psychiatrist, who had not himself seen the subjects, reviewed the records and assigned the ratings. (3) These difficulties led to a serious sampling bias. Since for lack of information the psychiatrist-rater had to discard "about one third of the cases which had been diagnosed by examining physicians," the final rates for the noninstitutionalized were based on an unrepresentative sample of Baltimore's population (Commission on Chronic Illness, 1957, p. 96).

we can tentatively conclude that Negro psychosis rates, especially for schizophrenia and some organic psychoses, are higher than white rates.

If group data on psychosis are difficult to decipher, group data on neurosis are even more confusing. Most of these less serious mental abnormalities do not require institutionalization; particularly among lower-status Negroes, neurotic symptoms may often be ignored. Not surprisingly then, comparative group data on neurosis are somewhat contradictory. Neurosis incidence rates for first admissions to state hospitals are generally much higher for whites than Negroes (Williams and Carmichael, 1949), though this may merely reflect that only incapacitated Negroes are accepted. In addition, many neurotics receive treatment from private sources, and for economic reasons these individuals are predominantly white.

Service studies from World War II provide inconclusive evidence. Two Navy investigators reported less neuroticism among Negroes than whites (Gardner and Aaron, 1946; Hunt, 1947a), whereas an Army investigation reported more frequent "minor psychiatric illness" among Negroes (Ripley and Wolf, 1947). This discrepancy may be due in large measure to different health standards applied by the two services at induction centers, for there is reason to suspect that the Army's wartime requirements for Negro inductees were especially low.

Personality test results on neurotic measures generally do not reveal racial differentials comparable to those obtained on measures of psychotic trends. In fact, two MMPI studies found samples of white males scored significantly higher than comparable Negro males on a character-disorder scale of psychopathic personality trends (Caldwell, 1959; Hokanson and Calden, 1960). Two examples of this scale include: "I have not lived the right kind of life," and "My way of doing things is apt to be misunderstood by others." All told, we can tentatively conclude that the ratio of Negro to white neuroticism is not so great as for the psychoses; and for certain other conditions, such as character disorders, the Negro rate may actually be less than the white. The findings on suicide are more straightforward. Negroes commit suicide far less frequently than whites; the national nonwhite death rate from suicide, 1949 through 1951, was only 42% of the white rate (National Office of Vital Statistics, 1959).

What lies behind these racial differences in mental illness? Authorities agree that innate racial factors do not provide an adequate explanation. To be sure, genetic potential probably interacts with environmental circumstances to produce such severe conditions as schizophrenia; but there is no evidence to suggest that this genetic potential is differentially distributed among the races. Instead, it is generally reasoned that the genetic potential for mental illness is roughly the same among the world's larger populations, but that dissimilar situations trigger the potential to diverse degrees. This thinking holds with special force in comparisons between Negro and white Americans, since they possess a considerable proportion of common genes in their two gene pools (Glass, 1955). Thus, any distinct differences in mental illness between the two groups should be traceable to contrasting patterns of environmental triggering. And these contrasting environmental patterns are not hard to identify, for distinctions of *social class*[4] and poverty, on the one hand, and racial restrictions, on the other, play critical roles in mental illness.

Witness first the importance of class. Hollingshead and Redlich (1958), in their research for their book, *Social Class and Mental Illness*, found the patterns of treated mental illness among white lower-class patients in New Haven closely resemble those just described for Negro patients.[5] Treated psychosis, particularly schizophrenia, has a higher incidence and prevalence among the poor than the prosperous. By contrast, neurosis incidence rates do not vary by class, though neurosis prevalence rates are actually higher among the economically well-to-do. The type of neurotic diagnosis also varies by class. Lower-status patients more often "act out" their problems—in antisocial and hysterical reactions—while upper-status patients more often "act in"—in depressive and obsessive-compulsive reactions and character disorders.

Faris and Dunham's (1939) Chicago data indicated that social classes within the city's Negro population had markedly diverse mental disorder rates.[6] The reported incidence of different types of schizophrenia, in particular, varied; the Negro area nearest the downtown business district had a rate over 60% greater than that of a more middle-class Negro area. Not all studies have obtained such clear results with Negroes, but an incidence survey of Philadelphia Negroes disclosed that schizophrenia and mental illness in general were much less frequent among upper-status Negroes (Parker, Kleiner, and Eskin, 1962). A study of first admissions to the state mental hospitals of Ohio showed similar findings. With each race analyzed separately, Frumkin (1954) noted that higher rates

---

[4]Words defined in the Glossary (p. 173) are italicized the first time they appear in each paper.

[5]Only 6% of the lowest two classes analyzed in the New Haven study was Negro.

[6]Compared with whites, Negro Americans have significantly higher rates of schizophrenia than manic-depression. This coincides with the fact that both the New Haven and Chicago investigations found less correlation between class and manic-depression than between class and schizophrenia. In addition, Kallman's (1951) twin studies reveal a smaller genetic component for schizophrenia than for manic-depression. In short, environmental factors appear more important for the mental disorder that reveals the greater racial differential.

existed for both the white and Negro lower classes. He concluded that the higher admission rates of Negroes were a "function of the low status of the Negro rather than some biological or genetic difference due to 'race.'"

But social class is only part of the explanation. As early as 1913, Arrah Evarts (1913) pointed out how the behavior of three Negro schizophrenics was directly related to their racially restricted experiences. These observations have often been repeated during the past half century. For example, a higher incidence of mental illness noted among Negro enlisted men on an isolated Pacific island was attributed by Ripley and Wolfe (1947) to, among other factors, the dissatisfaction of the Negroes with their white officers and their strong sense of being the victims of racial discrimination. The majority of the psychotic breakdowns among the Negroes in this situation were diagnosed as "paranoid schizophrenia," a fact that recalls the admonition of Kardiner and Ovesey (1951, p. 343) against hasty application of the term "paranoid" to Negro patients. For Negroes "to see hostility in the environment is a normal perception. Hence, we must guard against calling the Negro paranoid when he actually lives in an environment that persecutes him."

One of the less direct mechanisms whereby persecution might lead to greater mental illness is the necessity for persons with few job skills to migrate long distances to seek employment. There has been considerable controversy over this point; it now seems that previous waves of particularly poor Negro migrants did have unusually high rates of mental illness, as for example, during the 1930s, but that better-educated recent arrivals to the North no longer evince this phenomenon (Kleiner and Parker, 1959; Malzberg and Lee, 1956). Another possible mechanism is the perception of relative deprivation, the discrepancy between high aspirations and actual attainments. There is a growing body of research evidence that suggests this is a critical psychological determinant of mental disorder (Kleiner and Parker, 1963). And certainly racial discrimination acts to bar the very achievements that the society encourages individuals to attempt.

The deterioration of mental health through a combination of poverty and persecution is not limited to Negro Americans. The Peruvian mestizo, barely managing to survive on the out-skirts of Lima, presents a case in point (Rotondo et al., 1960). Mental illness, alcoholism, and family disorganization are widespread, as well as the familiar personality syndrome of inferiority feelings, insecurity, and hostility. The human species reacts to crushing oppression in much the same way the world over.

Also instructive is the comparison of data on Negro Americans with those on Jewish Americans. Rather than the near-total rejection long faced by Negroes, Jews have generally faced a more subtle, ambiguous kind of rejection. This more uncertain, shadowy form of discrimination, together with the Jews' higher social status and closer group and family bonds, have contributed to a mental illness pattern strikingly different from that of the Negro. Whereas the Negro suffers from psychosis relatively more than neurosis, Jews in the United States have fairly low psychosis rates but especially high neurosis rates (Myers and Roberts, 1958).

These Jewish patterns suggest a laboratory analogy. In his famous conditioning research on dogs, Ivan Pavlov established what appeared to be a type of "experimental neurosis." First, he trained a dog to distinguish between a circle and an ellipse by presenting food each time the circle appeared and withholding food each time the ellipse appeared. Then Pavlov began gradually altering the shape of the ellipse till it more and more resembled the circle. Suddenly, at a point when the hungry animal could no longer differentiate one object from another, the dog's behavior changed drastically. To speak anthropomorphically, the dog rejected the whole situation, became aggressive toward the experimenter, and in other ways tried to defend himself from intolerable anxiety. Other investigators, using an assortment of animals ranging from goats to chimpanzees, have replicated Pavlov's results. The "experimental neurosis" created by these researchers often has the long-term effects and stubborn resistance to therapy characteristic of the more serious human neuroses.

The subtleties of anti-Semitic discrimination often blur cues for the victim. Determining whether a cool reception represents bad manners or prejudice can be as difficult as distinguishing the circle from the modified ellipse. With legal desegregation, this kind of anxious uncertainty increases for the Negro. The clear-cut rejection of the past contributed to such conditions as the excessive withdrawal of schizophrenia; the ambiguous, discreet rejection of the future may well lead to an increase of neuroticism among Negroes, as it has among Jews. This possibility, along with the Negro's rising economic levels and strengthening group and family bonds, suggests a hypothesis for future trends in mental illness: among Negro Americans, phychosis rates will begin to recede as neurosis rates climb steadily.[7]

---

[7]Support for this hypothesis can be inferred from the findings of Myers and Roberts (1959), who compared the development of neurotics with that of schizophrenics in two social classes. Neurotics had been more rebellious and more often had come from stable homes and had loving and affectionate parents.

INTELLIGENCE

Even more popular attention has centered upon the other focus of the celebrated 1840 census—intelligence. But this realm is also complex.

Consider the often-cited Tanser (1939) study of intelligence among the Negro and white children of Kent County, Ontario, Canada. Tanser found that his white sample contained a higher average I.Q. than his Negro sample; but such results must be subjected to careful scrutiny. As in investigations in the United States, the social and economic conditions of Tanser's two groups were not equal. One psychologist, Mollie Smart, was born and raised in Kent County at approximately the time Tanser conducted the study there. She candidly describes the condition of the Negroes in this period (Smart, 1963, p. 621).

> Nearly all of the Negroes' houses were small wood buildings, often lacking paint and tending towards dilapidation. The theaters had a policy of seating Negroes in certain areas. The all-Negro school had been abandoned by my day. My elementary school classes always included Negro children, but I remember none during the last 3 years of high school. My Negro classmates were usually poorly clothed and badly groomed. Negroes held the low-status jobs. There were the servants, garbage collectors, and odd-job men. People called them "Nigger" more often than "Negro." I did not know until I grew up that a Negro could be a doctor, lawyer, teacher, member of Parliament, or even a clerk in a store . . . I cannot conceive of any social advantages which Negroes enjoyed in Kent County at the time of the Tanser study.

Tanser himself admitted that his sample of Negro children had not attended school as regularly as the white children. Moreover, it cannot be said that southern Ontario is free of racial prejudice and discrimination. Ever since the close of the American Civil War, the position of the Canadian Negro has steadily declined, with violent outbursts against Negroes occurring in Kent County itself (Franklin, 1961). The racial differences in I.Q. observed by Tanser, then, cannot be interpreted apart from the area's racial situation.

These difficulties point up the severely limiting methodological problems that confront this research realm. Any test of native intelligence must of necessity assume equivalent backgrounds of the individuals and groups under study. But until conditions entirely free from segregation and discrimination are achieved and the floor of Negro economic status is raised to the level of whites, the definitive research on racial differences in intelligence cannot be performed. Meanwhile, psychologists must conduct their work in a culture where training and opportunity for the two groups are never completely equal.

Empirical efforts are also hampered by the operation of selective factors in sampling. That is, Negroes and whites in the same situation—such as those inducted into the armed forces—may have been selected differently on intelligence, thus biasing the comparison of test scores between the two groups. For instance, Hunt (1947b) found that the Navy during World War II did not employ the same screening and selection standards for the two groups, permitting a far higher proportion of mental defectives among Negro than among white acceptances. Such a finding renders any comparisons in test scores between Negro and white sailors of dubious value. Much has been made of the intelligence test performances of the two "races" in both World Wars I and II, but such selective factors make these data difficult to interpret.

Despite these limitations, however, modern psychology has managed to achieve significant theoretical and empirical advances in this realm. These advances strongly favor a nongenetic interpretation of the typically lower intelligence test score averages of Negro groups. This work can be conveniently summarized under four general rubrics: (1) new theoretical conceptions; (2) the mediators of intellectual underdevelopment; (3) varying opportunities and group results; and (4) the individual versus the group.

New Theoretical Conceptions

Since World War II, psychologists and other scientists have seriously reviewed earlier notions about such basic concepts as "the environment," "heredity," and "intelligence." Instead of the older nature versus nurture concept, the emphasis is placed on nature and nurture.[8] Rather than asking which set of factors—environmental or hereditary—contributes more to a particular trait or ability, like intelligence, investigators ask how the environment and heredity combine to form the observed characteristic. *Genes* not only set broad limits on the range of development, but also enter into highly complex interactions with the environment, interactions which have not been emphasized enough in the past.

An ingenious animal experiment by Cooper and Zubek (1958) illustrates this genetic-environmental interaction. These investigators employed two genetically distinct strains of rats, carefully bred for 13 generations as either "bright" or "dull." Separate groups of the two strains

---

[8]Much of the following discussion is based on Gottesman's (1963) study.

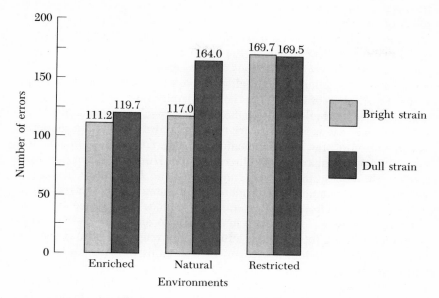

Figure 1. *Maze error scores for genetically bright and dull rats reared in three contrasting environments.*

grew up after weaning in three contrasting environments: a restricted environment, consisting of only a food box, water pan, and otherwise barren cage; a natural environment, consisting of the usual habitat of the laboratory rat; and an enriched environment, consisting of such objects as ramps, swings, slides, polished balls, tunnels, and teeter-totters plus a decorated wall beside their cages. Figure 1 shows the maze-learning performances of the six groups of rats (the fewer the errors, the more "intelligent" the behavior). Note that the two genetically diverse groups did almost equally well in the enriched and restricted environments, sharply differing only in the natural situation.[9] In fact, the environment masks genetic potential to the point where it is impossible to distinguish the enriched dulls from the natural brights or the natural dulls from the restricted brights.

The data of Figure 1 bear important implications. *Genotypes,* the true genetic potential, often do not coincide with *phenotypes,* the actual, expressed trait. Similar genotypes may have different phenotypes (e.g.,

[9]It should be noted, however, that these rats had been bred as "bright" or "dull" originally in the natural environment.

the bright rats in the restricted and enriched environments), and similar phenotypes may have different genotypes (e.g., the restricted bright and dull rats). Any phenotype is the composite product of the genotype and the environment in which the genetic potential must be realized. Relevant *nature-nurture* questions thus become: "How environmentally modifiable is the phenotypic intelligence of each genotype?" and "What is the contribution of heredity to the intelligence score differences among a group of individuals on a specific test in a specified environment?"

This newer view of the nature-nurture controversy and a mounting accumulation of new developmental evidence has resulted in a revised conception of the nature of intelligence. J. M. Hunt (1961) presents this modern thinking in his volume, *Intelligence and Experience*. Taking his cue from the strategies for information processing that are currently programmed for electronic computers, Hunt defines intelligence as central neural processes which develop in the brain to mediate between the information coming into the individual via the senses and the return signals for motor reaction. Moreover, he maintains that the initial establishment and subsequent capacity of these processes are probably rooted in the child's earliest encounters with the world around him. Intelligence, then, is not merely an inherited capacity, genetically fixed and destined to unfold in a biologically predetermined manner. It is a dynamic, on-going set of processes that within wide hereditary limits is subject to innumerable experiential factors.

Hunt's view upsets two long-unquestioned dogmas about intelligence, dogmas critical in the area of race differences. He terms them the assumptions of "fixed intelligence" and "predetermined development." The first of these has its roots in Darwin's theory of natural selection. Indeed, the assumption of fixed intelligence became so established before World War II that many psychologists regarded all evidence of substantial shifts in I.Q. as merely the product of poor testing procedures. But, objected Stoddard (1943, p. 281), "to regard all changes in mental status as an artifact is to shut one's eyes to the most significant and dramatic phenomenon in human growth."

The second assumption of "predetermined development" refers to the idea that, barring extreme interference from the environment, intelligence will unfold "naturally" with gene-determined anatomical maturation. Classic work on salamanders and Hopi Indian children was cited to demonstrate this maturation effect and that prior experience was unnecessary for normal development (Coghill, 1929; Dennis, 1940). In this era, mothers were told to avoid over-stimulating their children, to allow their children simply to grow "on their own." Hunt considers such advice "highly unfortunate," for it now appears that a proper matching of a child's development with challenging encounters with his environment is a critical requisite for increasing ability.

Notice that this new outlook in no way denies a hereditary influence on intelligence, an influence well established by twin studies (Gottesman, 1963). Rather, it views intelligence in much the same way that longevity is now regarded. A strong hereditary component is recognized in longevity; consistently long or short life spans typify many families. Yet, despite this component, the life expectancies at birth of Americans have almost doubled in the past century (Metropolitan Life Insurance Company, 1963). Better medical care, better diets, and a host of other environmental factors converge to enable Americans to make fuller use of their longevity potential. Likewise, the modern view of intelligence holds that we have not begun to expand our phenotypic intelligences even close to our genotypic potentials. From this vantage point, it appears that our society has placed too much emphasis on personnel selection at the expense of effective training programs.

Some of the most imaginative experimentation behind this new thinking is that of the eminent Swiss psychologist, Jean Piaget (1947). His ingenious and detailed studies with children of all ages provide abundant evidence that intelligence is the very antithesis of a fixed, predetermined capacity. And a wide range of other types of investigations amply bear out this conclusion. Even animal intelligence seems to be importantly affected by environmental opportunities. The previously-cited rat work of Cooper and Zubek (1958) shows how diverse cage environments affect later learning. In addition, pet-reared rats and dogs, with backgrounds of richly variegated experience, later evidence considerably more intelligent behavior than their cage-reared counterparts (Thompson and Melzack, 1956). And Harlow (1949) has demonstrated that monkeys can "learn to learn"; that is, they can develop learning sets which enable them to solve general classes of problems almost at a glance.

Similar effects of early environmental enrichment on the intelligence of young children have been noted. Kirk (1958) has shown that early educational procedures can often produce sharp increments in intellectual functioning among mentally retarded children, sometimes even among those diagnosed as organically impaired. Other studies on normal children, both white and Negro, suggest that preschool training in nursery and kindergarten classes may act to raise I.Q.'s (Anastasi, 1958, pp. 200–205; Deutsch and Brown, 1964; Hunt, 1961, pp. 27–34; Lee, 1951). Among criticisms of this research is the contention that a selection factor could be operating. The natively brighter children may be those who tend to have preschool education. But among deprived children in an orphanage, the beneficial results of early schooling have been noted in a situation where selection factors did not operate (Wellman and Pegram, 1944). Also relevant is the tendency for orphans to gain in I.Q. after adoption into superior foster homes, the gain being greatest for those adopted youngest (Freeman et al., 1928).

After reviewing research on cognitive learning in these early years, Fowler (1962) concludes that this is the period of human "apprenticeship." The infant is acquiring the most elementary and basic discriminations needed for later learning; like Harlow's monkeys, the infant is "learning to learn." Fowler speculates that conceptual learning sets, interest areas, and habit patterns may be more favorably established at these early stages than at later stages of the development cycle. Indeed, emphasis on "practical," concrete, gross motor learning in these early years may even inhibit later abstract learning.

In any event, research has documented the intellectually damaging consequences of deprived environments. An English study found that the children of such isolated groups as canal-boat and gypsy families achieved exceptionally low intelligence test scores, scores considerably below those typically found among Negro American children (Gordon, 1923). Interesting, too, is the fact that as these children grow older their I.Q.'s generally decline, though this is not the case for children of more privileged groups. In a similar fashion, children in orphanages and other institutions tend to have lower I.Q.'s and more retarded motor and linguistic development than children in stimulating home environments. Once again selection factors may operate, with the brighter, more developed children being more often chosen for adoption. However, studies that overcome much of this difficulty still note this institutional retardation (Brodbeck and Irwin, 1946; Dennis, 1960; Gilliland, 1949).

A related finding concerns the trend toward lower I.Q.'s of children raised in large families (Anastasi, 1956). One common explanation of this phenomenon is simply that parents who have large families are natively less intelligent. Yet, as Hunt (1961) points out, other findings strongly suggest that it is partly because parents of large families have less time to spend with each child. Thus, twins and doubles born close together in otherwise small families reveal a similar tendency toward lower I.Q.'s. And the negative relationship between family size and intelligence does not appear among wealthy families who can afford servants to provide stimulating attention for each child.

Finally, the extreme effects that can ensue from an impoverished environment are dramatically illustrated in a series of sensory deprivation experiments (Bexton, Heron, and Scott, 1954). These investigations reveal that normal people respond with marked psychological disturbances when severely restricted in activity and stimulation. They typically experience temporal and spatial distortions and pronounced hallucinations; and they evidence sharply impaired thinking and reasoning both during and after their isolation.

The Mediators of Intellectual Underdevelopment

Within this new perspective on intelligence as a relatively plastic quality, a series of environmental mediators of the individual Negro child's intellectual underdevelopment has been determined. In fact, these mediators exert their effects even upon the Negro fetus. One study found that dietary supplementation by vitamins supplied during the last half of pregnancy had directly beneficial effects on I.Q. scores of the children later (Harrell, Woodyard, and Gates, 1956). In a sample of mothers from the lowest socioeconomic level, 80% of whom were Negro, the group fortified with iron and vitamin B complex had children whose mean I.Q. at three years of age averaged five full points above the children of the unfortified control group, 103.4 to 98.4. One year later, the mean difference had enlarged to eight points, 101.7 to 93.6. The same researchers failed to find a similar effect among white mothers and their children from a mountain area. Presumably, the largely Negro sample was even poorer and more malnourished than the white sample from the mountains. Dire poverty, with its concomitant inadequate diet, can thus impair intelligence before the lower-class Negro child is born.

Economic problems also hamper intelligence through the mediation of premature births (Knobloch and Pasamanick, 1962). Premature children of all races reveal not only a heightened incidence of neurologic abnormalities and great susceptibility to disease, but also a considerably larger percentage of mental defectives (Harper, Fischer, and Rider, 1959; Knobloch et al., 1959). Another organic factor in intelligence is brain injury in the newborn. And both of these conditions have higher incidences among Negroes because of their greater frequency in the most economically depressed sectors of the population.

Later complications are introduced by the impoverished environments in which most Negro children grow up. At the youngest preschool ages, race differences in I.Q. means are minimal. Repeated research shows that in the first two years of life there are no significant racial differences in either psychomotor development or intelligence (Gilliland, 1951; Knobloch and Pasamanick, 1953; Pasamanick, 1946). And three later investigations provide convincing evidence that such properly administered infant tests predict later scores (Drillien, 1959; Hurst, 1963; Knobloch and Pasamanick, 1960). Furthermore, two northern investigations show little or no Negro lag in intellectual development through kindergarten and five years of age when thorough socioeconomic controls are applied (Anastasi and D'Angelo, 1952; Brown, 1944).

It is only after receiving a few years of inferior schooling that many Negro children drop noticeably in measured I.Q. (Osborn, 1960; Tomlinson, 1944). Part of this drop is due to the heavier reliance placed by intelligence tests at these ages upon verbal skills, skills that are particularly influenced by a constricted environment. One southern study of "Verbal Destitution" discovered that those Negro college students most retarded in a reading clinic came from small, segregated high schools and exhibited language patterns typical of the only adult models they had encountered—poorly educated parents, teachers, and ministers (Newton, 1960).

Another factor in the declining test averages over the school years is simply the nature of the schools themselves. Deutsch (1960, p. 3) gives the example of an assignment to write a page on "The Trip I Took," given to lower-class youngsters in a ghetto school who had never been more than twenty-five city blocks from home. Psychologist Deutsch maintains: "The school represents a foreign outpost in an encapsulated community which is surrounded by what, for the child, is unknown and foreign."

This tendency of the measured I.Q.'s of Negro children to diminish with increasing age is also noted among environmentally-deprived Caucasian groups—mountain and other rural children in America and the canal-boat and gypsy children in England. Furthermore, the positive relationship between socioeconomic status and tested I.Q. among Negroes increases with age, again suggesting that environmental factors become ever more vital as the child matures (Tomlinson, 1944).

The nature of the disrupted family life of many lower-status Negro youths decreases further the slum's environmental stimulation. Most of these youngsters are reared in large families, with reduced parental contact. And many of them are in fatherless homes. Deutsch (1960) and Stetler (1959) have both demonstrated that Negro children raised in such broken homes score significantly below comparable Negro children from intact homes on intelligence measures.

Other research pinpoints the tasks tested by intelligence tests which are most impaired by this restriction of stimulation. Woods and Toal (1957) matched two groups of Negro and white adolescents on I.Q. and noted subtest differences. While superior to the whites on some tests, the Negroes were noticeably deficient on tasks such as detection of errors and drawing pictorial completions which required spatial visualization. A series of similar studies reach the same conclusion (Davidson et al., 1950; Hammer, 1954; Newland and Lawrence, 1953). Machover (1943) demonstrated that this difficulty with perceptual and spatial relations was considerably more marked in a southern-reared Negro sample than in an I.Q.-matched northern-reared Negro sample. This breakdown of spatial performance among otherwise intelligent Negro children, especially in the more restrictive South, offers a suggestive parallel with the comparable spatial breakdown noted in the sensory-deprivation research. In any event, two additional studies provide evidence that this disability is correctable (Boger, 1952; Eagleson, 1937). Both studies gave groups of Negro and white children special training in spatial perception and found that the Negro subjects benefited more from the practice. I.Q. test scores were markedly higher for the Negro subjects five months after the training (Boger, 1952). Test authority Anne Anastasi (1958) believes this work supports the idea that the Negroes tested suffered from an unusually barren perceptual experience in early life.

Organic complications and environmental impoverishment are not the only mediators depressing Negro American intelligence scores. Both the "functioning intelligence" and the measured I.Q. of an individual are inseparably intertwined with his personality (Kagan et al., 1958; Sontag et al., 1955; Stringer, 1959). Edith Weisskopf (1951) has given case evidence of the great variety of ways personality problems can deter normal intellectual development. A child may do poorly in learning situations in a conscious or unconscious desire to punish his parents, to inflict self-punishment, or to avoid self-evaluation. And Roen (1960) has demonstrated that such personality problems are more highly related to intelligence test scores among Negroes than among whites. He equated two racial groups of soldiers on a wide range of social variables and found that a series of personality measures were more closely correlated with intelligence for the Negroes than for the whites. In particular, he noted that Negro soldiers who had low intelligence scores rated especially low on a self-confidence questionnaire.

Insecurity is especially provoked by any direct comparison with white performance. One investigation administered a task to southern Negro college students with two different sets of instructions (Katz et al., unpublished). One set told how other students at their college did on the task, while the second told how whites throughout the nation did. Those subjects who anticipated white comparison performed significantly more poorly on the task and indicated stronger concern and anxiety about their performance.

The role of "Negro" is a critical factor. Put simply, the Negro is not expected to be bright. To reveal high intelligence is to risk seeming "uppity." And once more the self-fulfilling prophecy begins to operate, for the Negro who assumes a facade of stupidity as a defense mechanism against oppression is very likely to grow into the role. He will not be eager to learn, and he will not strive to do well in the testing situation. After all, an intelligence test is a middle-class white man's instrument; it is a device whites use to prove their capacities and get ahead in the white world. Achieving a high test score does not have the same meaning for a lower-status Negro child, and it may even carry a definite connotation of personal threat. In this sense, scoring low on intelligence measures may for some talented Negro children be a rational response to perceived danger.

In addition to stupidity, the role of "Negro" prescribes both passivity and lack of ambition as central traits. And these traits are crucial personality correlates of I.Q. changes in white children. The Fels Research Institute found that aggressivenes and intense need for achievement differentiate those children whose scores rise between six and ten years of age from those whose scores recede (Kagan et al., 1958).

Another protective device is slowness. This trait assumes major importance in the speed instruments typically employed to estimate intelligence. In the Negro lower class there is no premium on speed, for work is generally paid by the hour and, realistically, there are few goals that fast, hard endeavor can attain. One experiment noted that differences in speed of response are primarily responsible for racial differences in I.Q. estimated by timed performance tests (Davidson et al., 1950).

Playing "Negro" is made especially critical when the examiner is white. Even two-year-old Negroes seem verbally inhibited when tested by a white (Pasamanick and Knobloch, 1955). In fact, this verbal inhibition may be the principal factor underlying the common observation that Negro children generally evidence verbal comprehension superior to their verbal communication (Carson and Rabin, 1960). Canady (1936) had students of both races tested alternately by Negro and white examiners. For both groups, the mean I.Q. was approximately six points higher when the test was administered by an examiner of their own race.

Adult Negroes evidence a similar reaction. A public opinion poll in North Carolina asked Negro respondents for the names of the men who had just run for governor in a primary election (Price and Searles, 1961). Three out of five Negroes questioned by Negro interviewers knew at least two correct names and gave no incorrect names, compared with only two out of five of a similar sample questioned by whites. A Boston survey replicated these results with two measures tapping intelligence (Pettigrew, unpublished). The first consisted of six informational items; each respondent was asked to identify six famous men: two Africans

(Kwame Nkrumah and Haile Selassie) and the rest Negro Americans (Louis Armstrong, Martin Luther King, Adam Clayton Powell, and Elijah Mohammad). The other test required synonyms for ten words, ranging in difficulty from "space" to "emanate." Negro interviewers questioned half of the respondents, and white interviewers the other half. The two samples were equivalent in income, age, education, and region of birth. Figure 2 presents the results. Note that on both tests the Boston Negro adults rendered more correct answers when interviewed by a Negro.

Apart from the role of "Negro," the middle-class bias of intelligence testing situations operates to hinder a disproportionate share of Negro examinees. Children perform best in situations familiar to them, but the conditions best suited for lower-status children are seldom attained. Most I.Q. tests are strictly urban middle-class instruments, with numerous references to objects and situations unfamiliar to rural and lower-class people. Haggard (1954) showed that a less middle-class-oriented test led to significant increases in the performances of lower-class children.

Tests are only one aspect of class bias, however. Middle-class students

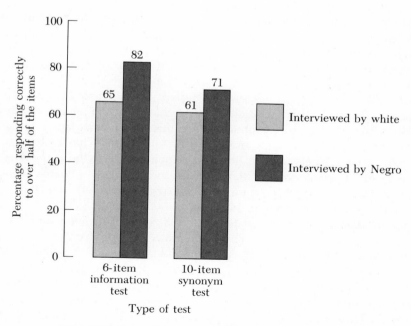

Figure 2. *Race of interviewer and Negro test performance.*

have generally internalized their need to excel at such tasks; a high test score is itself a reward. Moreover, they perform most competently in silent testing atmospheres that place heavy reliance upon reading skills. By contrast, lower-class students frequently require tangible, external rewards for motivation. And their typically restricted home environments are overwhelmingly dominated by the spoken, rather than the written, word. It is not surprising, then, that Haggard (1954) discovered notable increments in intelligence test scores of lower-class children when there was extra motivation for doing well (e.g., a prize of movie tickets) and when the questions were read aloud as well as written. Sophisticated testing in ghetto schools should follow such guidelines for more adequate estimates of the abilities of disadvantaged children.

Varying Opportunities and Group Results

If all of these mechanisms are operating to mediate the influence of a lean, hostile, and constricted environment upon the individual Negro's tested intelligence, certain group trends under conditions of varying opportunities can be predicted. These testable hypotheses are (1) in environments that approach being equally restrictive for children of both races, the intelligence test means of both will be low and will approach equality; (2) in environments that approach being equally stimulating for children of both races, the intelligence test means of both will be high and will approach equality; and (3) when any racial group moves from a restrictive to a comparatively stimulating environment, its measured I.Q. mean will rise.

The first of these hypotheses was tested on an isolated Caribbean island, offering little stimulation to its youth. It had "no regular steamship service, no railroad, motion picture theater, or newspaper. There were very few automobiles and very few telephones. The roads were generally poor. There were no government schools above the elementary level and no private schools above the secondary level . . . People of all colors, then, were restricted to a rather narrow range of occupational opportunity" (Curti, 1960, p. 14).

Even here, however, complete equality of status between whites and Negroes was not achieved. White skin was "highly respected," whites typically held the better jobs; and while almost half of the white students attended private schools, nine-tenths of the Negroes attended government schools. Nevertheless, there were no significant color differences on nine of the fourteen intelligence measures. The Negroes did best on tests which were less class-linked, less threatening, and less dependent on uncommon words. Thus, socioeconomic status was a more important factor than race on four of the five instruments that did yield racial discrepancies, and "lack of confidence," as rated independently by teachers, was highly related to three of them. In general, the island youngsters scored rather low on the tests, with race a relatively insignificant consideration. And the selective migration possibility that the brighter whites were leaving the island is not an explanation for these findings, since there was apparently little emigration or immigration. These data, gathered in a locality that approached being equally restrictive for both races, do "not lend support to the conclusion that colored inferiority in intelligence tests has a racial basis" (Curti, 1960, p. 26).

The second hypothesis has also received support from a number of studies. Three investigations, testing young children in Minneapolis (Brown, 1944), grade-school students in a Nevada city (McQueen and Churn, 1960), and adolescents in the Boston area (McCord and Demerath, 1958), revealed that, once social-class factors are rigorously controlled, there are only minor black-white mean I.Q. differences. In these relatively stimulating, educationally-desegregated urban communities, both racial groups secured test averages equal to the national norms.

Thus, I.Q. means of groups are retarded where there are constrictive environmental conditions and elevated where there are at least average conditions. Three ecological projects provide further evidence for this generalization. One project correlated home rentals with the I.Q. averages of the school children in 300 New York City neighborhoods (Maller, 1933). Moderately high and positive relationships were found; the more expensive the neighborhood, the higher the test scores. Another noted very close and positive associations between such variables as per capita income and the mean I.Q. level of sixth-grade pupils in 30 American cities (Thorndike and Woodyard, 1942). The third project discovered that these ecological correlations tend to be higher for intelligence scores than for scholastic achievement, demonstrating again the extreme sensitivity of the measured I.Q. to the total social environment (Thorndike, 1951).

This research is confirmed by other investigations conducted exclusively among Negroes (Deutsch and Brown, 1964; Roberts, 1948; Robinson and Meenes, 1947), especially since World War II and its attendant expansion of social-class differentiation among Negro Americans. Socioeconomic variables correlate highly and positively with I.Q. ranges in Negro samples. For example, the I.Q. means of groups of Negro third-graders in Washington, D.C., tended to be highest in areas where radios were most often present in the homes and where rents were highest.

These results suggest the third hypothesis: when any group moves from a restrictive to a comparatively stimulating environment, its measured I.Q. mean will rise. Dramatic evidence for this proposition comes from the unique situation of the Osage Indians. Like many other Indian groups, the Osage were granted land for the establishment of a reservation. Oil was later discovered on their land, and the Osage became relatively prosperous. Since the Osage had not chosen their land, the oil discovery was not an indication of native ingenuity beyond that of Indian groups in general. But now they could afford living standards vastly superior to other Indians, and on both performance and language tests they were found to meet the national norms and to have achieved the level of comparable whites in the area (Rohrer, 1942). This finding is all the more impressive when it is remembered that Indian children generally have measured considerably below Negro children in I.Q. tests.

Similar improvements are recorded among white mountain children in east Tennessee, public school students in Honolulu, and white enlisted men in World War II. Wheeler (1942) gave tests to over 3,000 mountain children in 1940 and compared their performance to that of children in the same areas and from virtually the same families in 1930. This ten-year span had witnessed broad economic, social, and educational changes in east Tennessee; and the median I.Q.'s reflected these changes in an increment of 11 points, from 82 to 93. Equally remarkable gains are reported for children of many racial groups in Honolulu after a 14-year period of steady improvement in the city's schools (Smith, 1942). And, finally, 768 soldiers, representative of white enlisted men in World War II, took the old Army Alpha verbal test of World War I and provided striking evidence of the nation's rising intelligence between the two wars. Tuddenham (1948) shows that the typical white World War II enlisted man did better on the test than 83% of the enlisted men of World War I.

Once the Negro American escapes from inferior conditions, his improved performance parallels that of the Osage Indians and the east Tennessee mountain children. Service in the armed forces is one of the most important sources of wider experience and opportunities for Negroes, including those who are illiterate. The Army in the Second World War operated Special Training Units and provided a basic fourth-grade education in eight weeks for 254,000 previously illiterate soldiers— roughly half of them Negroes and the great majority southerners. A slightly higher percentage of the Negroes than whites successfully completed the intensive course, though how this bears on larger questions of Negro intelligence is a matter of debate, since the men given this special training were selected. There is no debate, however, over the fact that the success of these units proves the educability of many apparently retarded men of both races (Bradley, 1949; Witty, 1945).

Another mode of improvement for many Negroes is to migrate North. Northern Negroes routinely achieve higher test medians than comparable southern Negroes (Davenport, 1946; Roberts, 1948). And Negro children born in the North achieve higher medians than those who come to the North from the South (Klineberg, 1935; Lee, 1951; Long, 1934; Stetler, 1959). But do the Negro children who migrate improve their group performance as they remain in the North? This was the central question the eminent psychologist Otto Klineberg (1935) set out to answer in what resulted in perhaps the best known research in the field of race differences. Over 3,000 ten-to-twelve-year-old Harlem Negroes took an array of individual and group intelligence tests. These data clearly indicate that the longer the southern-born children had resided in New York City, the higher their intelligence scores. Those who had been in the North for a number of years approached the levels attained by the northern-born Negroes. Smaller studies with less elaborate designs obtained parallel results in Cleveland and Washington, D.C. (Dombey, 1933; Long, 1934).

Lee (1951) replicated these findings in Philadelphia with the most rigorous research on the topic to date. Employing large samples in a variety of different schools, Lee analyzed the test scores of the same children as they progressed through the city's school system. Though never quite catching up with the Philadelphia-born Negro students, the southern Negro migrants as a group regularly gained in I.Q. with each grade completed in northern schools. And the younger they were when they entered the Philadelphia school system, the greater their mean increase and final I.Q. The effects of the more stimulating and somewhat less discriminatory North, then, are directly reflected in the measured intelligence of the youngest of Negro migrants.

The major complication in interpreting the Klineberg and Lee work is again introduced by possible selection biases. Those Negro southerners who migrate North in search of a better life may be selectively brighter and rear brighter children. But other possibilities also exist. Many of the more intelligent Negroes in the South gain some measure of success and establish roots that are more difficult to break than those of the less intelligent. This phenomenon would operate to make the Klineberg and Lee data all the more impressive. Or, perhaps, intelligence has little or nothing to do with the decision to migrate; personality traits, such as aggressiveness or inability to control hostility over racial frustrations, may be more decisive. In any event, Klineberg (1935) found the southern school grades of 562 Negro youths who had since gone North were typical of the entire Negro school populations from which they migrated. More research is needed, but it seems that selective migration cannot begin to account for the dramatic improvement in test performance demonstrated by Negro children who move to the North.

Further evidence that Negro ability goes up when environmental opportunities expand derives from the many diverse educational-enrichment programs current in our major cities. The best known of these is New York City's "Higher Horizons" project. This effort provides a selected and largely Negro student body with an expensive saturation of skilled specialists: remedial-reading teachers, guidance counselors, psychologists, and social workers. Its results have been striking; in the first year, the program cut third graders' retardation in reading from six months down to a single month. Backed by major foundation grants, other cities have also begun to experiment. Detroit and Philadelphia tried sending "school-community agents" into ghetto schools in an attempt to win parental support for education. Kansas City's Central High School and Tucson's Pueblo High School initiated imaginative new programs. And Washington, D.C., launched in 1959 a "talent search" project for 200 deprived seventh graders, 92% of whom were Negro. Similar to Higher Horizons in its concentration of staff and exposure of students to new cultural experiences, the "talent search" was soon declared a success. Contrasted with a matched control group, the students of the program showed a sharply reduced scholastic failure rate and notable instances of I.Q. increments.

Perhaps the most remarkable demonstration of all is Samuel Shepard's "Banneker Group" work in St. Louis (Baron, 1963; Silberman, 1962). A forceful educator, Shepard performs his "miracles" on the most underprivileged school children in the city without the vast expenditures of other efforts. The Banneker Group consists of 23 elementary schools, with over 16,000 slum and public housing children, more than 95% of them Negro. A Negro who overcame serious economic disadvantages himself, Shepard adamantly rejects the old dogma that substandard school work is all you can realistically expect from ghetto children. He bluntly challenges the pupils, parents, principals, and teachers of the district to perform up to national standards; he appeals to race pride and resorts to continuous exhortations, rallies, contests, posters, and meetings with teachers and parents. Students who make good grades are asked to stand in assemblies for the applause of their classmates. Teachers are asked to visit the homes of their charges. And parents are asked to provide their offspring with encouragement, study space, a library card, a dictionary, and other books as gifts. As a concrete incentive, Shepard points out the new and better jobs now open to Negroes in St. Louis and the lack of qualified Negroes to fill them.

The results of the Banneker effort speak for themselves. Despite an unending stream of poorly educated migrants into the area from the South, all test indicators have risen. In the first four years of the program, the median I.Q. increased from the middle 80s to the 90s; median reading, language, and arithmetic levels all climbed; and the percentage of Banneker graduates accepted for the top-ability program in St. Louis's desegregated high schools tripled.

The striking results of these imaginative demonstrations may not be due directly to the exact procedures introduced. Given their vast variety of techniques and their uniform success, the demonstrations probably achieve most of their gains because of the sheer fact of intervention—any kind of thoughtful intervention. Often the rate of initial progress slows once the beginning enthusiasm cools. But this is irrelevant to the larger issue of Negro American intelligence. Dramatic improvement in Negro performance for whatever reason is evidence of the underlying potential for learning heretofore stifled by lack of opportunity and attention. This potential for learning is also evident in the findings of an experiment at the University of Texas (Semler and Iscoe, 1963). Negro children learned series of paired material as rapidly and well as white children, even though they came from lower socioeconomic backgrounds and had significantly lower I.Q.'s.

Such demonstrations arouse speculation concerning the effects of desegregation of public school systems. Segregationists have long voiced the unsubstantiated opinion that "school mixing" would mean educational chaos with the Negroes dragging down the higher white standards. But the experience of a great diversity of communities indicates that these fears are unjustified. Administrators of 17 desegregated school systems appeared before the United States Civil Rights Commission in March, 1959, and candidly discussed their problems (Southern Regional Council, 1960). Twelve of the educators dealt with the question of academic standards. Ranging from Logan County, Kentucky, and Muskogee, Oklahoma, to Baltimore and Nashville, all twelve reported unequivocally that their academic standards had not been lowered—in fact, many maintained that their standards had improved for both races.

Washington, D.C., provided the acid test. It embarked upon a sweeping process of educational desegregation in 1954 with Negroes comprising three-fifths of the students, many of them from the South, with limited backgrounds. A four-tract system of ability grouping and other innovations were adopted. Five years later, in 1959, a factual assessment of the changes were made (Hansen, 1960; Stallings, 1960). Though Negro students, swelled by migrants, now comprised three-fourths of the student body, achievement test scores had risen significantly for each grade level sampled, and each subject area tested approached or equaled national norms. Furthermore, both Negro and white students shared in these increments. Such results are not unique to Washington. Louisville reported substantial gains in Negro performance and slight gains in white performance after only one year of desegregation (Southern Regional Council, 1959; Stallings, 1959).

Clearly, desegregation per se does not accomplish these feats. The Banneker demonstration in St. Louis took place in virtually all-Negro schools; Washington, D.C., and Louisville witnessed sharply improved test medians among their Negro students, whether in biracial or uniracial schools. The principal factor seems to be the new and healthier self-image Negroes acquire in the process. The act of community desegregation bolsters and encourages Negro pupils, parents, and teachers alike. Combining with this heightening of morale is the entrenched Negro desire for education. *Newsweek's* (1963) national poll revealed that 97% of the nation's Negroes want their children at least to graduate from high school.

Also important is the sudden interest Negro education finally wins from the whole community. As long as Negro education is a racially separate system, dominant white interests can and do forget it. But once desegregation forces the community to handle the education of its youth in one package, to consider Negro education as an integral part of the whole process, new attention is given to the schools. Indeed, the rise in white test scores after desegregation suggests that public education as a whole benefits from the greater public interest. Washington, D.C., offers an illustration. Prior to desegregation, survey testing was only done with the white pupils; Negroes were ignored (Southern Regional Council, 1960). But immediately after desegregation, testing throughout the system was insituted, and the same standards were applied at last to both races. Certainly, desegregation is no panacea for the immense problems faced by public school systems with large percentages of environmentally impoverished children, but it does prepare the way for tackling the real problems of modern education.

Thus, an array of stimulating circumstances—service in the armed forces, migration to the North, and participation in revitalized school systems—all act to lift substantially the intelligence and achievement levels of Negroes. Often these improvements still do not bring the average Negro performance completely up to white norms, but this cannot be considered as evidence for genetic racial differences until *all* racial discrimination is abolished.

The Individual Versus the Group

The discussion so far has concentrated on group results; yet many of the most important considerations involving Negro American intelligence concern the individual. No one denies the existence of outstanding Negro Americans. Usually, however, the same individuals are cited—Marian Anderson, Ralph Bunche, George Washington Carver—and are considered "exceptions" and special "credits to their race." The truth is that a surprising number of such "exceptional" Negroes have somehow managed to overcome the formidable obstacles of discrimination. Many have naturally entered the struggle for equal rights. But others achieve such stature in nonstereotyped work that they are no longer thought of as a Negro. For instance, the originator of the Hinton test for syphilis, the late Professor William A. Hinton, was well known as a bacteriologist and immunologist at Harvard Medical School, but not as a Negro.

Superior intelligence comes in all skin colors. While the intelligence test means of the two races are still divergent, the range of performance—from the most retarded idiot to the most brilliant genius—is much the same in the two groups. Some Negro children score I.Q.'s into the gifted range (130 or over) and up to 200 (Jenkins, 1948; Theman and Witty, 1943; Witty and Jenkins, 1936). To be sure, the frequency of such bright Negroes is less than that of whites, but this, too, can be explained by differential environmental factors. The great majority of these superior Negroes are located in biracial schools in the urban North and West, which suggests that many potentially gifted Negroes go either undiscovered or undeveloped in the segregated schools of the South (Jenkins, 1948; Jenkins and Randall, 1948). Proof that such children do exist in the South comes from programs that intensively seek talented Negro southerners (Clark, 1956; Stalnaker, 1948). Once found, they receive scholarships and attend a variety of desegregated high schools and colleges in the North, and the great majority of them accommodate well to their new and challenging situations. Indeed, a recent study of Negro scholarship applicants from the South who have attended integrated colleges reveals that they have a far smaller dropout rate than white students at the same colleges (Clark and Plotkin, 1963).

Moreover, it appears that the degree of white ancestry does not relate to Negro I.Q. scores (Herskovits, 1926; Klineberg, 1928). Among intellectually superior Negroes, for example, the proportions of those with varying degrees of white ancestry correspond closely to those of the

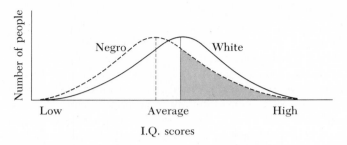

Figure 3. *Typical test distributions with "25% overlap" (shaded area).*

total Negro American population (Witty and Jenkins, 1936). Indeed, the brightest Negro child yet reported—with a tested I.Q. of 200—had no traceable Caucasian heritage whatsoever (Theman and Witty, 1943). "Race per se," concludes Martin Jenkins (1948, p. 401), "is not a limiting factor in psychometric intelligence."

There exists, then, a considerable overlap in the I.Q. distributions of the two groups. A few Negroes will score higher than almost all Caucasians, and many Negroes will score higher than most Caucasians. Figure 3 shows two typical intelligence test distributions with an overlap of 25%, that is, 25% of the Negroes tested (shaded area) surpass the performance of half of the whites tested. Notice how the ranges of the two distributions are virtually the same, even though the means are somewhat different. This figure illustrates one of the most important facts about "race" and measured intelligence: individual differences in I.Q. within any one race greatly exceed differences between races.

There are two practical consequences of this phenomenon for desegregated education. First, when a school system institutes a track program of ability grouping, there will be Negroes and whites at all levels. Second, some gifted Negroes will actually lead their biracial classes even during the initial stages of desegregation. Thus, Janice Bell, a seventeen-year-old Negro girl, led the first graduating class of superior students at Beaumont High in St. Louis; Julius Chambers, a twenty-four-year-old Negro southerner, became the 1961-1962 editor of the University of North Carolina's *Law Review* in recognition of his leadership of his law school class; and Charles Christian, a thirty-seven-year-old Negro Virginian, led his Medical College of Virginia senior class academically in 1962. "In the study of individuals," summarizes Anastasi (1958), "the only proper unit is the individual."

THE CURRENT CONCLUSION

Intelligence is a plastic product of inherited structure developed by environmental stimulation and opportunity, an alloy of endowment and experience. It can be measured and studied only by inference, through observing behavior defined as "intelligent" in terms of particular cultural content and values. Thus, the severely deprived surroundings of the average Negro child can lower his measured I.Q. in two basic ways. First, it can act to deter his actual intellectual development by presenting him with such a constricted encounter with the world that his innate potential is barely tapped. And, second, it can act to mask his actual functioning intelligence in the test situation by not preparing him culturally and motivationally for such a middle-class task. "Only a very uncritical psychologist would offer sweeping generalizations about the intellectual superiority or inferiority of particular racial or ethnic groups," comments Tuddenham (1962, pp. 499–500), "despite the not very surprising fact that members of the dominant racial and cultural group in our society ordinarily score higher than others on tests of socially relevant accomplishments invented by and for members of that group."

The principal mechanisms for mediating these environmental effects vary from the poor nutrition of the pregnant mother to meeting the expectations of the social role of "Negro." Some of these mechanisms, like fetal brain injuries, can leave permanent intellectual impairments. Consequently, the permanency and irreversibility of these effects are not, as some claim, certain indicators of genetically low capacity. Fortunately, many of these effects are correctable. Moving North to better schools, taking part in special programs of environmental enrichment, and benefiting from challenging new situations of educational desegregation can all stimulate Negro children to raise their I.Q. levels dramatically.

From this array of data, the overwhelming opinion of modern psychology concludes that the mean differences often observed between Negro and white children are largely the result of environmental, rather than genetic, factors. However, this is *not* to assert that psychologists deny altogether the possibility of inherited racial differences in intellectual structure. Psychology is joined in this conclusion by its sister behavioral sciences: sociology and anthropology. Witness the following professional statements.

The Society for the Psychological Study of Social Issues, a division of the American Psychological Association, concluded in 1961:

There are differences in intelligence test scores when one compares a random sample of whites and Negroes. What is equally clear is that no evidence exists that leads to the conclusion that such differences are innate. Quite to the contrary, the evidence points overwhelmingly to the fact that when one compares Negroes and whites of comparable cultural and educational backgrounds, differences in intelligence diminish markedly; the more comparable the background, the less the difference. There is no direct evidence that supports the view that there is an innate difference between members of different racial groups. . . . Evidence speaks for itself and it casts serious doubt on the conclusion that there is any innate inequality in intelligence in different racial groups . . . .

The Society for the Study of Social Problems, a section of the American Sociological Association, concurred, in the same year:

The great preponderance of scientific opinion has favored the conclusion that there is little or no ground on which to assume that the racial groups in question are innately different in any important human capacity . . . the conclusion of scientists is that the differences in test performance are due not to racial but to environmental factors. This is the operating assumption today of the vast majority of the competent scientists in the field . . . .

The American Anthropological Association passed a resolution by a unanimous vote (192 to 0) in 1961:

The American Anthropological Association repudiates statements now appearing in the United States that Negroes are biologically and in innate mental ability inferior to whites, and reaffirms the fact that there is no scientifically established evidence to justify the exclusion of any race from the rights guaranteed by the Constitution of the United States. The basic principles of equality of opportunity and equality before the law are compatible with all that is known about human biology. All races possess the abilities needed to participate fully in the democratic way of life and in modern technological civilization.

The final, definitive research must await a racially integrated America in which opportunities are the same for both races. But, ironically, by that future time the question of racial differences in intelligence will have lost its salience; scholars will wonder why we generated so much heat over such an irrelevant topic.

The important conclusion for the present, however, is that if there are any inherent distinctions, they are inconsequential. Even now, differences in I.Q. within any one race greatly exceed the differences between the races. Race as such is simply not an accurate way to judge an individual's intelligence. The real problems in this area concern ways to overcome the many serious environmental deprivations that handicap Negro youth. To return to the analogy with longevity, the problem is akin to that which faced medicine in the nineteenth century. Automatized America needs to expand the intelligence level of its underprivileged citizens in much the same way it has expanded the life potential of its citizens in the past one hundred years. The success of such programs as the Banneker Group in St. Louis demonstrates that this job can be accomplished when American society decides to put enough of its resources into it. "The U.S. must learn," writes Charles Silberman (1962, p. 151) in *Fortune*, "to look upon the Negro community as if it were an underdeveloped country."

REFERENCES

Anastasi, A. 1956. Intelligence and family size. *Psychol. Bull.* 53: 187–209.

Anastasi, A. 1958. *Differential psychology*, 3rd ed. New York: Macmillan.

Anastasi, A., and R. D'Angelo. 1952. A comparison of Negro and white preschool children in language development and Goodenough Draw-A-Man I.Q. *J. Genet. Psychol.* 81: 147–165.

Baron, H. 1963. Samuel Shepard and the Banneker Project. *Integrated Educ.* 1 (April): 25–27.

Bexton, W. H., W. Heron, and T. H. Scott. 1954. Effects of decreased variation in the sensory environment. *Canad. J. Psychol.* 8: 70–76.

Boger, J. H. 1952. An experimental study of the effects of perceptual training on group I.Q. test scores of elementary pupils in rural ungraded schools. *J. Educ. Res.* 46: 43–52.

Bradley, G. 1949. A review of educational problems based on military selection and classification data in World War II. *J. Educ. Res.* 43: 161–174.

Brodbeck, A. J., and O. C. Irwin. 1946. The speech behavior of infants without families. *Child Develop.* 17: 147–156.

Brown, F. 1944. An experimental and critical study of the intelligence of Negro and white kindergarten children. *J. Genet, Psychol.* 65: 161–175.

Caldwell, M. G. 1959. Personality trends in the youthful male offender. *J. Crim. Law, Criminol., and Police Sci.* 49: 405–416.

Canady, H. G. 1936. The effect of "rapport" on the I.Q.: A new approach to the problem of racial psychology. *J. Negro Educ.* 5: 209–219.

Carson, A. S., and A. I. Rabin. 1960. Verbal comprehension and communication in Negro and white children. *J. Educ. Psychol.* 51: 47–51.

Clark, K. B. 1956. The most valuable hidden resource. *Coll. Board Rev.* 29: 23–26.

Clark, K. B., and L. Plotkin. 1963. *The Negro student at integrated colleges.* National Scholarship Service and Fund for Negro Students, New York.

Coghill, G. E. 1929. *Anatomy and the problem of behavior.* New York: Macmillan.

Commission on Chronic Illness. 1957. *Chronic illness in the United States,* Vol. IV. *Chronic illness in a large city: The Baltimore study.* Cambridge, Mass.: Harvard Univ. Press.

Cooper, R. M., and J. M. Zubek. 1958. Effects on enriched and constructed early environments on the learning ability of bright and dull rats. *Canad. J. Psychol.* 12: 159–164.

Crawford, F. R. G., W. Rollins, and R. L. Sutherland. 1960. Variations between Negroes and whites in concepts of mental illness and its treatment. *Ann. N. Y. Acad. Sci.* 84(17): 918–937.

Curti, M. W. 1960. Intelligence tests of white and colored school children in Grand Cayman. *J. Psychol.* 49: 13–27.

Davenport, R. K. 1946. Implications of military selection and classification in relation to universal military training. *J. Negro Educ.* 15: 585–594.

Davidson, K. S., R. G. Gibby, E. B. McNeil, S. J. Segal and H. Silverman. 1950. A preliminary study of Negro and white differences in Form I of the Wechsler-Bellevue scale. *J. Consult. Psychol.* 14: 489–492.

Dennis, W. 1940. The effect of cradling practices upon the onset of walking in Hopi children. *J. Genet. Psychol.* 56: 77–86.

Dennis, W. 1960. Causes of retardation among institutional children: Iran. *J. Genet. Psychol.* 96: 47–59.

Deutsch, M. 1960. *Minority group and class status as related to social and personality factors in scholastic achievement.* Society for Applied Anthropology, Monograph no. 2, pp. 1–32.

Deutsch, M., and B. Brown. 1964. Social influences in Negro-white intelligence differences. *J. Soc. Issues* 20(2): 24–35.

Dombey, E. H. 1933. A comparison of the intelligence test scores of southern and northern born Negroes residing in Cleveland. Unpublished Master's Thesis, Western Reserve University.

Drillien, C. M. 1959. Physical and mental handicap in prematurely born. *J. Obstet. Gynaec. Brit. Comm.* 66: 721–728.

Eagleson, O. W. 1937. Comparative studies of white and Negro subjects in learning to discriminate visual magnitude. *J. Psychol.* 4: 167–197.

Evarts, A. B. 1913. Dementia praecox in the colored race. *Psychoanal. Rev.* 1: 388–403.

Faris, R. E. L., and H. W. Dunham. 1939. *Mental disorders in urban areas.* Chicago: Univ. Chicago Press.

Fowler, W. 1962. Cognitive learning in infancy and early childhood. *Psychol. Bull.* 59: 116–152.

Franklin, J H. 1961. *From slavery to freedom,* 2nd ed. New York: Knopf.

Freeman, F. N., K. J. Holzinger, and B. C. Mitchell. 1928. The influence of environment on the intelligence, school achievement, and conduct of foster children. *27th Yearbook, Nat. Soc. Social Sci. Educ.* Part I: 103–217.

Friedsam, H. J., C. D. Whatley, and A. L. Rhodes. 1954. Some selected aspects of judicial commitments of the mentally ill in Texas. *Texas J. Sci.* 6: 27–30.

Frumkin, R. M. 1954. Race and major mental disorders: A research note. *J. Negro Educ.* 23: 97–98.

Gardner, G. E., and S. Aaron. 1946. The childhood and adolescent adjustment of Negro psychiatric casualties. *Amer. J. Orthopsychiat* 16: 481–495.

Gilliland, A. R. 1949. Environmental influences on infant intelligence test scores. *Harvard Educ. Rev.* 19: 142–146.

Gilliland, A. R. 1951. Socioeconomic status and race as factors in infant intelligence test scores. *Child Develop.* 22: 271–273.

Glass, B. 1955. On the unlikelihood of significant admixture of genes from the North American Indians in the present composition of the Negroes of the United States. *Amer. J. Hum. Genet.* 7: 368–385.

Gordon, H. 1923. *Mental and scholastic tests among retarded children.* Board of Education (Educational Pamphlet No. 44), London.

Gottesman, I. I. 1963. Genetic aspects of intelligent behavior. In N. Ellis, ed., *The handbook of mental deficiency.* New York: McGraw-Hill. Pp. 253–296.

Haggard, E. A. 1954. Social status and intelligence: An experimental study of certain cultural determinants of measured intelligence. *Genet. Psychol. Monogr.* 49: 141–186.

Hammer, E. F. 1954. Comparison of the performances of Negro children and adolescents on two tests of intelligence, one an emergency scale. *J. Genet. Psychol.* 84: 95–98.

Hansen, C. F. 1960. *Addendum: A five-year report on desegregation in the Washington, D.C. schools.* Anti-Defamation League of B'nai B'rith, New York.

Harlow, H. F. 1949. The formation of learning sets. *Psychol. Rev.* 56: 51–65.

Harper, P. A., L. K. Fischer, and R. V. Rider. 1959. Neurological and intellectual status of prematures at three to five years of age. *J. Pediat.* 55: 679–690.

Harrell, R. F., E. R. Woodyard, and A. I. Gates. 1956. Influence of vitamin supplementation of diets of pregnant and lactating women on intelligence of their offspring. *Metabolism* 5: 555–562.

Herskovits, M. J. 1926. On the relation between Negro-white mixture and standing in intelligence tests. *Pediat. Sem.* 33: 30–42.

Hokanson, J. E., and G. Calden. 1960. Negro-white differences on the MMPI. *J. Clin. Psychol.* 16: 32–33.

Hollingshead, A. B., and F. C. Redlich. 1958. *Social class and mental illness: A community study.* New York: Wiley.

Hunt, J. M. 1961. *Intelligence and experience*. New York: Ronald.

Hunt, W. A. 1947a. The relative incidence of psychoneurosis among Negroes. *J. Consult. Psychol.* 11: 133–136.

Hunt, W. A. 1947b. Negro-white differences in intelligence in World War II— A note of caution. *J. Abnorm. Soc. Psychol.* 42: 254–255.

Hurst, J. G. 1963. Relationships between performance on preschool and adult intelligence measures. Paper presented at the Annual Meeting of the American Psychological Association, held at Philadelphia in August.

Ivins, S. P. 1950. Psychoses in the Negro: A preliminary study. *Delaware State Med. J.* 22: 212–213.

Jaco, E. G. 1960. *The social epidemiology of mental disorders*. New York: Russell Sage Foundation.

Jenkins, M. D. 1948. The upper limit of ability among American Negroes. *Sci. Mon.* 66: 399–401.

Jenkins, M. D., and C. M. Randall. 1948. Differential characteristics of superior and unselected Negro college students. *J. Soc. Psychol.* 27: 187–202.

Kagan, J., L. W. Sontag, C. T. Baker, and V. Nelson. 1958. Personality and I.Q. change. *J. Abnorm. Soc. Psychol.* 56: 261–266.

Kallman, F. J. 1951. Twin samples in relation to adjustive problems of man. *Trans. N.Y. Acad. Sci.* 13: 270–275.

Kardiner, A., and L. Ovesey. 1951. *The mark of oppression*. New York: Norton.

Katz, I., E. G. Epps, and L. J. Axelson. The effects of anticipated comparison with whites and with other Negroes upon the digit-symbol performance of Negro college students. Unpublished paper.

Kirk, S. A. 1958. *Early education of the mentally retarded*. Urbana: Univ. Illinois Press.

Kleiner, R. J., and S. Parker. 1959. Migration and mental illness: A new look. *Amer. Soc. Rev.* 24: 687–690.

Kleiner, R. J., and S. Parker. 1963. Goal-striving, social status, and mental disorder: A research review. *Amer. Soc. Rev.* 28: 189–203.

Klineberg, O. 1928. An experimental study of speed and other factors in "racial" differences. *Arch. Psychol.* No. 93.

Klineberg, O. 1935. *Negro intelligence and selective migration*. New York: Columbia Univ. Press.

Knobloch, H., and B. Pasamanick. 1953. Further observations on the behavioral development of Negro children. *J. Genet. Psychol.* 83: 137–157.

Knobloch, H., and B. Pasamanick. 1960. Environmental factors affecting human development before and after birth. *Pediatrics* 26: 210–218.

Knobloch, H., and B. Pasamanick. 1962. Mental subnormality. *New Eng. J. Med.* 266: 1092–1097.

Knobloch, Hilda, R. Rider, P. Harper, and B. Pasamanick. 1959. Effect of prematurity on health and growth. *Amer. J. Public Health* 49: 1164–1173.

Lee, E. S. 1951. Negro intelligence and selective migration: A Philadelphia test of the Klineberg hypothesis. *Amer. Soc. Rev.* 16: 227–233.

Litwack, L. F. 1961. *North of slavery.* Chicago: Univ. Chicago Press.

Long, H. H. 1934. The intelligence of colored elementary pupils in Washington, D.C. *J. Negro Educ.* 3: 205–222.

Machover, S. 1943. Cultural and racial variations in patterns of intellect. *Teachers Coll. Contrib. to Educ.*, no. 875.

Maller, B. 1933. Mental ability and its relation to physical health and social economic status. *Psychol. Clin.* 22: 101–107.

Malzberg, B. 1944. Mental disease among American Negroes: A statistical analysis. In O. Klineberg, ed., *Characteristics of the American Negro.* New York: Harper. Pp. 373–395.

Malzberg, B. 1953. Mental disease among Negroes in New York State, 1939-1941. *Mental Hyg.* 37: 450–476.

Malzberg, B. 1956. Mental disease among native and foreign-born Negroes in New York State. *J. Negro Educ.* 25: 175–181.

Malzberg, B. 1959. Mental disease among Negroes: An analysis of first admissions in New York State, 1949-1951. *Mental Hyg.* 43: 422–459.

Malzberg, B., and E. S. Lee. 1956. *Migration and mental disease.* Social Science Research Council, New York.

McCord, W. M., and N. J. Demerath, III. 1958. Negro versus white intelligence: A continuing controversy. *Harvard Educ. Rev.* 28: 120–135.

McQueen, R., and B. Churn. 1960. The intelligence and educational achievement of a matched sample of white and Negro students. *Sch. Soc.* 88: 327–329.

Metropolitan Life Insurance Company. 1963. Progress in longevity since 1850. *Stat. Bull.* 44: 1–3.

Myers, J. K. 1959. *Family and class dynamics in mental illness.* New York: Wiley.

Myers, J. K., and B. H. Roberts. 1958. Some relationships between religion, ethnic origin and mental illness. In M. Sklare, ed., *The Jews: Social patterns of an American group.* Glencoe, Ill.: Free Press.

National Office of Vital Statistics. 1959. *Death rates for selected causes by age, color, and sex: United States and each state, 1949-1951.* Washington, D.C.: U.S. Government Printing Office.

Newland, T. E., and W. C. Lawrence. 1953. Chicago non-verbal examination results on an East Tennessee Negro population. *J. Clin. Psychol.* 9: 44–46.

Newsweek editors. 1963. The Negro in America. *Newsweek* 62 (July 29): 15–34.

Newton, Eunice. 1960. Verbal destitution: The pivotal barrier to learning. *J. Negro Educ.* 24: 497–499.

Osborn, R. T. 1960. Racial differences in mental growth and school achievement: A longitudinal study. *Psychol. Reports* 7: 233–239.

Parker, S., R. J. Kleiner, and R. M. Eskin. 1962. Social status and psychopathology. Paper presented at the Annual Meeting of the Society of Physical Anthropology, held in Philadelphia in April.

Pasamanick, B. 1946. A comparative study of the behavioral development of Negro infants. *J. Genet. Psychol.* 69: 3–44.

Pasamanick, B. 1963. Some misconceptions concerning differences in the racial prevalence of mental disease. *Amer. J. Orthopsychiat.* 33: 72–86.

Pasamanick, B., and H. Knobloch. 1955. Early language behavior in Negro children and the testing of intelligence. *J. Abnorm. Soc. Psychol.* 50: 401–402.

Pettigrew, T. F. The Negro respondent: New data on old problems. Unpublished paper.

Piaget, J. 1947. *The psychology of intelligence.* Translated by M. Piercy and D. E. Berlyne. London: Routledge and Kegan Paul.

Postell, W. D. 1953. Mental health among the slave population of southern plantations. *Amer. J. Psychiat.* 110: 52–54.

Price, D. O., and R. Searles. 1961. Some effects of interviewer-respondent interaction on responses in a survey situation. Paper presented at the Annual Meeting of the American Statistical Association, held in New York, December 30.

Ripley, H. S., and S. Wolf. 1947. Mental illness among Negro troops overseas. *Amer. J. Psychiat.* 103: 499–512.

Roberts, S. O. 1948. Socioeconomic status and performance on the ACE of Negro freshmen college veterans and non-veterans, from the North and South. *Amer. Psychol.* 3: 266.

Robinson, M. L., and M. Meenes. 1947. The relationship between test intelligence of third grade Negro children and the occupations of their parents. *J. Negro Educ.* 16: 136–141.

Roen, S. R. 1960. Personality and Negro-white intelligence. *J. Abnorm. Soc. Psychol.* 61: 148–150.

Rohrer, J. H. 1942. The test intelligence of Osage Indians. *J. Soc. Psychol.* 16: 99–105.

Rotondo, U., C. B. Vigil, C. G. Pachecho, J. Mariategui, and B. DeDegaldo. 1960. Personalidad básica: Dilemas y vida de familia de un grupo de mestizos. *Rev. Psicol.* (Lima) 2: 3–60.

Schermerhorn, R. A. 1956. Psychiatric disorders among Negroes: A sociological note. *Amer. J. Psychiat.* 112: 878–882.

Semler, I. J., and I. Iscoe. 1963. Comparative and developmental study of the learning abilities of Negro and white children under four conditions. *J. Educ. Psychol.* 54: 38–44.

Silberman, C. E. 1962. The city and the Negro. *Fortune* 65: (March): 89–91, 139–154.

Smart, M. S. 1963. Confirming Klineberg's suspicion. *Amer. Psychol.* 18: 621.

Smith, S. 1942. Language and nonverbal test performance of racial groups before and after a 14-year interval. *J. Genet. Psychol.* 26: 51–93.

Sontag, L. W., C. T. Baker, and V. Nelson. 1955. Personality as a determinant of performance. *Amer. J. Orthopsychiat.* 25: 555–562.

Southern Regional Council. 1959. Did you find that there was much difference in the ability of Negro children to receive and profit by instruction? *Report No. L-13*, December 15.

Southern Regional Council. 1960. Desegregation and academic achievement. *Report No. L-17*, March 14.

Stallings, F. H. 1959. A study of the immediate effects of integration on scholastic achievement in the Louisville public schools. *Negro Educ.* 28: 439–444.

Stallings, F. H. 1960. Racial differences and academic achievement. *Southern Regional Council's Report No. L-16*, February 26.

Stalnaker, J. M. 1948. Identification of the best southern Negro high school seniors. *Sci. Mon.* 67: 237–239.

Stanton, W. 1960. *The leopard's spots: Scientific attitudes toward race in America, 1815-1859*. Chicago: Univ. Chicago Press.

Stetler, H. G. 1959. *Comparative study of Negro and white dropouts in selected Connecticut high schools*. Connecticut Commission on Civil Rights, Hartford.

Stewart, D. D. 1955. Posthospital social adjustment of former mental patients from two Arkansas counties. *Southwest. Soc. Sci. Quart.* 35: 317–323.

Stoddard, G. D. 1943. *The meaning of intelligence*. New York: Macmillan.

Stringer, L. A. 1959. Academic progress as an index of mental health. *J. Soc. Issues* 15: 16–29.

Tanser, H. A. 1939. *The settlement of Negroes in Kent County, Ontario, and a study of the mental capacity of their descendants*. Chatham, Ontario: Shephard.

Theman, V., and P. A. Witty. 1943. Case studies and genetic records of two gifted Negroes. *J. Psychol.* 15: 165–181.

Thompson, W. R., and R. Melzack. 1956. Early environment. *Sci. Amer.* 194 (1): 38–42.

Thorndike, E. L., and E. Woodyard. 1942. Differences within and between communities in the intelligence of children. *J. Educ. Psychol.* 33: 641–656.

Thorndike, R. L. 1951. Community variables as predictors of intelligence and academic achievement. *J. Educ. Psychol.* 42: 321–338.

Tomlinson, H. 1944. Differences between preschool Negro children and their older siblings on the Stanford-Binet scales. *J. Negro Educ.* 13: 474–479.

Tuddenham, R. D. 1948. Soldier intelligence in World Wars I and II. *Amer. Pseuchol.* 3: 54–56.

Tuddenham, R. D. 1962. The nature and measurement of intelligence. In L. Postman, ed., *Psychology in the making.* New York: Knopf.

Weisskopf, E. 1951. Intellectual malfunctioning and personality. *J. Abnorm. Soc. Psychol.* 46: 410–423.

Wellman, B. L., and E. L. Pegram. 1944. Binet I.Q. changes of orphanage preschool children: A re-analysis. *J. Genet. Psychol.* 65: 239–263.

Wheeler, L. R. 1942. A comparative study of the intelligence of East Tennessee mountain children. *J. Educ. Psychol.* 33: 321–334.

Williams, E. Y., and C. P. Carmichael. 1949. The incidence of mental disease in the Negro. *J. Negro Educ.* 18: 276–282.

Wilson, D. C., and E. M. Lantz. 1957. The effect of culture change on the Negro race in Virginia as indicated by a study of state hospital admissions. *Amer. J. Psychiat.* 114: 25–32.

Witty, P. 1945. New evidence on the learning ability of the Negro. *J. Abnorm. Soc. Psychol.* 40: 401–404.

Witty, P., and M. D. Jenkins. 1936. Intra-race testing and Negro intelligence. *J. Psychol.* 1: 179–192.

Woods, W. A., and R. Toal. 1957. Subtest disparity of Negro and white groups matched for I.Q.'s on the revised Beta test. *J. Consult. Psychol.* 21: 136–138.

Poverty and inferior education are so interrelated as to form a single problem. And so long as poverty correlates with race, racial groups will differ in educational opportunity and thereby in education-based achievement. Motivation is also a prerequisite to success, and motivation for increased education requires an orientation toward the future and the rewards such education will eventually bring. As long as low-income people are oriented mainly to the present—often by necessity because of the daily problems their poverty poses—even equal opportunities for education will fail to remove inequalities in achievement.

The Disadvantaged Child: His Education and Life Chances

FRANCIS P. PURCELL
MAURIE HILLSON
Graduate School of Education
Rutgers University
New Brunswick, New Jersey

It is accepted by most that the royal road from poverty to affluence is through education. The two issues, poverty and inferior education, join as if a single problem. The attempt to mitigate poverty in this country has developed at the same time as the movement to obtain civil rights for the Negro minority in the United States. The latter, without doubt, has given tremendous impetus to the former, and the educational establishment has become the focal point of concern in each instance. Unfortunately, the problems of education for the disadvantaged have also become identified largely with education of Negro children. A substantial collection of evidence indicates that the phenomenon of *social class*,[1] not race or ethnicity, is the overriding factor to be considered in addressing these problems.

A recent study of 5,000 aid-to-dependent-children families disclosed

---

[1] Words defined in the Glossary (p. 173) are italicized the first time they appear in each paper.

a discouragingly high drop-out rate from school for these children. Their school retardation (index of relative performance for age and grade level) was twice that of the national average. Children in these families grew up to hold low-status employment, if employed at all. In this study, fewer than 7% had attained the level of skilled craftsmen. As a result, a second generation of aid-to-dependent-children families has arisen, and a third one is emerging (Burgess and Price, 1963). What factors operate to create such widespread poverty and dependency? Surely today it can be accepted that huge learning deficits occur in the children of such families, regardless of race; and because of this, they are not assimilated into the mainstream of American culture.

Failure of the educational system to enable and encourage youth from minority groups to take advantage of available opportunity is widely known. Evidence gathered by Sheldon and Glazier (1965) emphasizes the racial character of school failure. They note that in New York City not one school with 90% minority enrollment (Negro and Puerto Rican) attained the average sixth-grade reading scores, while 99% of the "white schools" were at grade level or above. Similar results were obtained when I.Q. scores were compared. Not a single "minority school" attained the mean I.Q. of 100 or higher. Two-thirds of the schools fell between I.Q. scores of 85 and 94, and one-third between 70 and 84. In comparison, 98% of the "white schools" had I.Q. scores of 100 or better.

Among the junior high schools, not a single "minority school" had a mean I.Q. score as high as 95, and 75% ranged between 70 and 84. In contrast, all the "white schools" averaged an I.Q. score of 100 or over. There was not a single "minority junior high school" where the eighth grade scored at the eighth-grade level; but 94% of the "white schools" scored at the normal level.

Wilson's (1963) comparative study of schools in California produced similar results with one major exception. The differences varied with social class. The same might be noted for the New York schools as well, rather than considering race as the major variable.

Wilson notes that "a continuously accumulating body of research over the past few decades has made it clear, however, that utilization of the educational opportunities follows, to a large degree, the lines of the stratification of the society." Furthermore, research has disclosed the mechanism that sustains "intergenerational inheritance" of positions within an educational system, indicating that social attitudes toward education by students are laterally diffused among their peers. For example, Wilson found that students from similar family backgrounds tended to correspond to the mode of the school in which they were enrolled. Thus, while 93% of the sons of professionals in predominantly upper white-collar schools said they wanted to go to college, only 64% of their peers who were enrolled in schools predominated by children of manual workers shared this aspiration. In the latter school, only one-third of the sons of manual workers hoped to go to college, while three-fifths of the manual workers' sons attending the largely white-collar school wanted to enter college (Wilson, 1963).

Attitudes that alienate children from the classroom learning are similarly diffused through the peer group relationship. In addition, it has been noted that lower-class children tend to be governed more by attitudes spread horizontally by their peers than are middle-class children who tend to adopt their attitudes in a vertical fashion from prestige-status adults around them.

Social attitudes that prevent academic achievement are easy enough to identify. But why do they withstand all efforts on the part of school and communities to modify them? As Kluckhohn (1960) points out, one reason may be that the school system in the United States is highly future-oriented, while the life style of low-income people is often oriented to the present. Achievement beyond that of "a sense of being" also represents a value difference. Children reared in one value system find the whole set of teaching and learning expectations of another system alien and even hostile. Other findings indicate that while our society promises occupational reward for academic achievement, a person's social origin, despite his education, can depress upward social mobility (Lipset and Bendix, 1959). Negro youth easily perceive that there are those among them who fail to compete successfully with whites with equal education.

Still other forces militate against academic achievement in low-income-area schools. Sexton (1961) notes that schools in low-income areas are older. They have fewer facilities for both recreation and education. Despite greater need, they are less likely to have remedial facilities. A greater proportion of the teaching time is provided by substitute teachers. Becker's (1958) study documents the fact that in Chicago, public school teachers initiate their careers in low-income neighborhoods where there are more vacancies, but transfer out as soon as possible. Cloward and Jones (1963) suggest that because of the high turnover of teachers and their lack of experience, along with the high geographic mobility of low-income persons, the youth from low-income areas receive less instructional time. Deutch's study (1960) indicates that in certain deprived areas, as much as 80% of the school day is devoted to discipline or organizational detail. Even the better teachers devoted 50% of their time to such activities.

If social class is a significant determinant in the learning process of individuals, then there should be measurable differences between children from different social classes within an ethnic group. As the age of the children increases, the measurable differences should also increase. In an effort to study the impact of early social environment on the patterning of intellectual skills in young children, John (1963) produced findings to support this contention. Negro children from lower-class, lower-middle-class, and middle-class families submitted to a variety of intellectual measurements. Middle-class children surpassed their lower-class age mates in vocabulary, nonverbal I.Q., and in a conceptual sorting activity. The differences in the performance of these tasks became statistically significant by the fifth-grade level, while they were less than significant at the first-grade level.

Countless studies have documented the eroding effect of slum life on the I.Q.'s of young children. In a study of the Harlem schools, Keller (1963) notes that average I.Q. scores decline from a normal 96.5 in the first grade to 88.5 in the fifth grade. By the time the child reaches the fifth grade, his grade reading level is two grades retarded. Some regard Negro reading retardation of "only" two years as remarkable. They wonder if some kind of superiority is not operant to enable these students to achieve so much in the face of the impossible obstacles that confront them. After reviewing the handicaps that Negroes face, Pettigrew (1964) muses whether the Negroes are not actually intellectually superior to whites, who do not achieve even greater margins of success with their environmental advantages. He cites numerous studies indicating the significance of social class variables in the comparison of Negro-white I.Q. scores. Other studies cited by Pettigrew indicate very strongly that I.Q. scores improve among all groups as the socioeconomic conditions improve.

What it is within the low-income culture that produces handicaps for learning is not entirely clear. Deutsch (1960) states that in his experience he has never seen a school curriculum specifically designed for the life styles and cognitive needs of low-income, socially deprived children. Deutsch's study indicates that in these deprived areas

> for the most part, the teachers felt alien to the community within which they worked, and with one or two exceptions, they themselves lived in other neighborhoods. Even though the teachers blamed the school administrators, charging that they had no appreciation of the special problems existing in the education of the lower-class, and most specifically the Negro

and Puerto Rican child, and were always imposing an educational orientation which was exclusively developed for a middle-class population who have very different preparations for learning, . . .

Davis (1951) has estimated that 95% of the school teachers in the United States are middle-class in their orientation. As a group, they achieve full-fledged middle-class status through their professional teacher education (Super, 1957). Schools organized and administered and taught against a backdrop of middle-class life concerns may inadvertently establish a culture-conflict situation, bringing with it corresponding ingroup-outgroup hostilities and alienations. When teachers on New York's lower East Side were provided with seminars stressing cultural theory and social behavior together with visits to the homes of their pupils, they were reported as becoming more accepting of suggested changes within the classroom and more appreciative of the severe problems families contended with in the inner-city slum. While the controls instituted in this experiment were not sufficiently maintained to produce significant measurable changes in attitude, teachers' testimony indicated that distinct changes in feelings occurred that produced a reduction in social distance.

The following description by a graduate student assigned to the Mobilization for Youth project in New York City lends substance to the foregoing (Brager, 1964). While this example is more clear-cut because of the language bias, similar culture-conflicts emerge whenever low-income children invade the classrooms of middle-class teachers.

> The purpose of the visit to this class was to listen to the children's oral language and read some of their written expression. The teacher attempted to evoke responses to an assembly program the children had just viewed, but was unsuccessful. In reacting to some responses, she indicated that there was a correct answer, predecided by her, and that approximations of it were unacceptable. This aroused hesitation and reluctance to speak on the part of many children, but the teacher's standard was maintained and, one might add, met, by her own responses to the question she posed.

It is evident that neurophysical processes cannot be held accountable for the educational deficits accruing among America's low-income population. Then what is it in the life experience of the child from a low-income area that produces adaptive responses leading to nonlearning in the classroom? A casual observation of the inner-city slum reveals noise, high density of people, run-down shops, garbage-littered streets, narcotic pushers, bookies, flagrant traffic violations, and overwhelming evidence of all kinds of civic disinterest. The disregard of adolescents obviously under the influence of alcohol and often tragically under the effects of heroin attests to adult indifference. Death on the streets is not uncommon. Ambulances and emergency vehicles rush to their destinations and are so commonplace that children do not look up from their play. One can also be impressed by the unlimited opportunity for social intercourse—untidy but cheerful children, miraculously avoiding injury by speeding automobiles; small coteries of people talking with great animation; the willingness to give directions or to ask for them. In the midst of despair, one can still easily perceive the warmth, spontaneity, and human directness of the people.

Another factor which Keller (1963) notes is that low-income children have less interaction with parents. They do not converse much with other adults as do middle-class children. Shared family activities are rare:

> Even at meal times, one half of these children are alone or in the company of their brothers and sisters. It is interesting to note that though these children are poor, they are not starving—the list of foods typically eaten at breakfast and at dinner includes a considerable variety of nutritionally adequate food, although food amounts were not indicated. Poverty, today, probably extends more to housing, to lack of spending money, to lack of comforts, and to a constricted milieu for learning and exploring the world. A city, especially a metropolis, would seem to be a fascinating place in which to grow up, but one would not believe this from the accounts of restricted movement and the monotonous repetitiveness of activities—TV and more TV, play with other children, movies, and, as the single organized activity besides school, church on Sunday for one-half of the group. Their world seems to be small and monotonous, though not necessarily an unhappy one.
>
> This constriction of experience and the poverty of spirit it engenders may account for the below normal I.Q. scores of this group of poor children by the time of the fifth grade (mean I.Q. is 88.57 on Lorge Thorndike nonverbal I.Q. test; in first grade, Lorge Thorndike I.Q. mean scores were 96.56) confirming countless other studies that have shown a similar scholastic and verbal inferiority for children from underprivileged environments. It may also account for the high degree of negative self-evaluation— more than half of the children in each grade feeling ashamed, sad, or peculiar when they draw comparisons between themselves and other children. And perhaps their lofty occupational choices are a sign of their discomfort with their crowded homes, their uneducated parents, the hit-and-run quality of their relations with their families, and the absence of constructive and exciting things to do and to learn outside of school. In any case, it is quite clear that a low self-esteem and a high occupational aspiration characterize these deprived urban children at this time.

Of the many factors that militate against the success of low-income children, one focal point of the problem centers on their communication skills and attendant language usage. Bernstein, an English sociologist, offers a viable sociolinguistic theory in which he sees language as the pivotal factor in socialization. He postulates the existence of two linguistic codes: elaborated and restricted. These, he contends, regulate behavior. They are used differently by social classes. Each code requires distinct verbal planning. The middle classes manipulate the verbal symbols successfully in the elaborated code. Conversely, the lower classes operate in a restricted code and are restricted by it to a different level of opportunity (Bernstein, 1961). Teachers generally deal with or speak an elaborated code. Theirs is a language, or verbalization scheme, representative of middle-class society.

A simple nontechnical analysis of what is normally done in the middle-class home could serve as a teacher job description as it outlines some of the methods which might be successfully employed in teaching the disadvantaged child. Bloom, Davis, and Hess (1965) reflect this idea clearly.

> The child in many middle-class homes is given a great deal of instruction about the world in which he lives, to use language to fix aspects of this world in his memory, and to think about similarities, differences, and relationships in this very complex environment. Such instruction is individual and is timed in relation to experiences, actions, and questions of the child. Parents make great efforts to motivate the child, to reward him, and to reinforce desired responses. The child is read to, spoken to, and is constantly subjected to a stimulating set of experiences in a very complex environment. In short, he "learns to learn" very early. He comes to view the world as something he can master through a relatively enjoyable type of activity, a sort of game which is learning. In fact, much of the approval he gets is because of his rapid and accurate response to his formal instruction at home.

To move from a disadvantaged life—the culture of poverty, failure, threat, instability, and insecurity—requires a self-conceptualization that allows for insight, with careful sociologically based guidance, into functionally realistic aspirational goals for all levels of existence (Kvaraceus et al., 1965). The idea must be that if the youngster tries and is given the opportunity for success, *he can make it!* He needs to be given the opportunities to rehabilitate all of the necessary personal equipment to handle his own life situation satisfactorily, with security and with success.

Wasted lives, wasted resources, and wasted talents are always frustrating. Can anyone disagree with the conclusion of the Rockefeller Panel Reports (1961, p. 380) that of all the categories of wasted talent "the one that must lie heaviest on our conscience is our disadvantaged minorities."

REFERENCES

Becker, H. 1958. The career of the Chicago public school teacher. *Amer. Sociol. Rev.* 17: 470–477.

Bernstein, B. 1961. Social class and linguistic development: A theory of social class learning. In A. H. Halsey, *Education, economy and society.* Glencoe, Ill.: Free Press.

Bloom, B. S., A. Davis, R. D. Hess, and S. Silverman. 1965. *Compensatory education for cultural deprivation.* New York: Holt, Rinehart, and Winston.

Brager, G. 1964. *Influencing institutional change through a demonstration project: The case of the schools.* Mobilization for Youth, Inc., New York. Mimeo.

Burgess, M. E., and D. D. Price. 1963. *An American dependency challenge.* Chicago: American Public Welfare Association.

Cloward, R. A., and J. A. Jones. 1963. Social class: Educational attitudes and participation. In A. H. Passow, ed., *Education in depressed areas.* New York: Bureau of Publications, Teachers College, Columbia University.

Davis, A. 1951. What are some of the basic issues in the relation of intelligence tests to cultural background? In K. Eells, *Intelligence and cultural differences.* Chicago: Univ. Chicago Press.

Deutsch, M. P. 1960. *Minority-group and class status as related to social and personality factors in scholastic achievement.* Monograph No. 2. New York: The Society for Applied Anthropology.

John, V. P. 1963. The intellectual development of slum children: Some preliminary findings. *Amer. J. Orthopsychiat.* 33: 813–822.

Keller, S. 1963. The social world of the urban slum child. *Amer. J. Orthopsychiat.* 33: 823–831.

Kluckhohn, Florence. 1960. Variations in the basic values of family systems. In N. W. Bell and E. F. Vogel, eds., *A modern introduction to the family.* New York: The Free Press.

Kvaraceus, W. C., J. S. Gibson, F. K. Patterson, and J. D. Grambs, eds. 1965. *Negro self-concept: Implications for school and citizenship.* New York: McGraw-Hill.

Lipset, S. M., and R. Bendix. 1959. *Social mobility in industrial society.* Berkeley and Los Angeles: Univ. California Press.

Pettigrew, T. F. 1964. *A profile of the Negro American.* Princeton: Van Nostrand.

Rockefeller Panel Reports, The. 1961. *The pursuit of excellence: Education and the future of America. Report #5.* New York: Doubleday.

Sexton, P. C. 1961. *Education and income: Inequalities of opportunity in our public schools.* New York: Viking Press.

Sheldon, E. B., and R. A. Glazier. 1965. *A fact book, New York.* New York: Russell Sage Foundation.

Super, D. 1957. *The psychology of careers.* New York: Harper.

Wilson, A. B. 1963. Social stratification and academic achievement. In A. H. Passow, ed., *Education in depressed areas.* New York: Bureau of Publications, Teachers College, Columbia University.

The birth rate of the nonwhite population of the United States is higher than that of the white population at all socioeconomic levels except the highest, where it drops below the white birth rate. Further data from the 1960 census also indicate that the fertility differentials are tied to age at marriage, housing, and education; the lower the level of any of the three, the higher the birth rate. The Growth of American Families Study of the attitudes, behavior, and background of couples that determine the number of children they desire, expect, and actually produce showed that the family-size ideals of nonwhite couples were actually lower than those of whites. Within the nonwhite population, those couples who live in the rural South or who have southern farm origins were found to have unusually high fertility, which tended to obscure the fact that nonwhite couples with no southern farm background had about the same number of births as white couples of similar education and socioeconomic status. Low educational levels were again found to correlate with higher birth rates among nonwhites.

Nonwhite Fertility and Family Planning

ARTHUR A. CAMPBELL
National Center for Health Statistics
Public Health Service
Washington, D.C.

CLYDE V. KISER
Milbank Memorial Fund
New York, New York

The nonwhite population of the United States has a substantially higher birth rate than the white population. Between 1951 and 1963 the crude birth rate of nonwhites varied between 30 and 34 per thousand while the rate of whites ranged between 21 and 24. For 1967 the rate was 25 for nonwhites and 17 for whites. However, such broad statistics provide no information about where the greatest and least fertility differentials exist within each population and suggest no guidelines for assessing probable future population trends. Age, socioeconomic status, region, urban or rural residence are all highly significant variables with each color group.

If we are going to examine population differences on the single criterion of color, the most logical first question is: What *ethnic groups*[1] comprise the nonwhite population of the United States and are there differences in birth rates among them? In the 1960 census some 92% of the people classified as "nonwhites" were Negroes; the remaining 8% were individuals of Japanese or Chinese birth or ancestry (3.5%), American Indians (2.7%), and Filipinos and others (1.9%). As for differences in birth rates, for ever-married[2] women under age 25 the fertility rates were higher for Negroes than other nonwhites. At the older ages of the child-bearing period, the rates were highest for American Indians. Women of Japanese or Chinese ancestry had the lowest fertility of nonwhites from ages 15 to 39 (see Kiser, Grabill, Campbell, 1968).

Since American Indians are chiefly rural and the Japanese and Chinese are chiefly urban, it is well to hold type of residence constant in making the comparisons by specific ethnic groups. Within either urban or rural areas, the fertility rates of Negroes surpassed those of other nonwhites at ages under 25. Negro and American Indian women had approximately equal fertility at ages 25–29. However, at ages 30–45 the Indians surpassed other nonwhites in fertility within "other than urbanized areas." At ages 45–49 in urban areas the fertility rates of Japanese and Chinese surpassed both Indians and Negroes. Women of these ages reflected the relatively low fertility rates of Negroes and the relatively high fertility rates of Orientals in cities a generation ago. In both urban and rural areas the fertility rates of Japanese women under forty years old tended not only to fall below that of other nonwhite groups, but also below that of white groups. Of related interest is the fact that the median number of years of school completed by Japanese women tended to outrank that of any other ethnic group of women of comparable age, including native whites.

Returning to our comparison of the white and nonwhite population as a whole, we find that between 1950 and 1960 the fertility differential between them increased at all ages of the child-bearing period, especially at ages 25–39. At these ages, the excess fertility of nonwhites over whites jumped from 19% in 1950 to 27% in 1960. In general, the percentage excess of fertility of nonwhites over whites continued to be greatest at the younger ages and least at the older ages. In 1960 it extended from 69% at ages 15–19 to 18% at ages 40–44. By type of community, the excess fertility of nonwhites was highest in rural areas, particularly the South, and lowest in urban areas.

---

[1]Words defined in the Glossary (p. 173) are italicized the first time they appear in each paper.

[2]*Ever-married* refers to those women who have ever been married, whether or not they are presently widowed or divorced.

The range of fertility rates by socioeconomic status tends to be wider among nonwhites than among whites. This holds to the extent that at the upper socioeconomic levels the fertility rates of nonwhite ever-married women over age 25 tended to be smaller than those of similar whites, while at the lower socioeconomic levels the fertility rates of nonwhites tended to surpass those of whites. Thus, in the United States as whole, or in urban areas considered separately, nonwhite women over age 25 reporting college attendance had fewer children on the average than did similar white women. This was also true for wives whose husbands had attended college, were professionals, or in the upper-income groups. However, it should be pointed out that the largest differential occurred when the educational attainment of the wives themselves was considered.

Census tabulations of fertility rates in relation to color, age, marriage age of wife, and three simultaneously considered indices of husband's socioeconomic status (education, occupation, and income) yielded several interesting situations. The data suggest that age at marriage is a critical factor in fertility differentials by both color and socioeconomic status. Among women marrying before age twenty-two, the predominant pattern is of higher fertility rates of nonwhites than whites, particularly at the lower socioeconomic levels. In contrast, among women marrying at ages twenty-two and over, the instances of lower fertility rates of nonwhites than of whites were found much more frequently and at lower levels of socioeconomic status than among those marrying at earlier ages. However, even among women marrying at ages twenty-two and over, the cases of lower fertility rates of nonwhite than of whites and the cases of direct relation of fertility to socioeconomic status tended to be more frequent in urban than in rural areas and more frequent in the upper than the lower levels of socioeconomic status.

Part of the reason for the lower fertility rates of nonwhite than of white women of college attainment is the relatively late age at marriage of this group, especially for those reporting four or more years of college. Late age at marriage apparently has more impact on the fertility rate of nonwhite women than on white women of college attainment. Studies have also indicated that among these women the higher proportion of broken marriages and the higher proportion of women in the labor force among the nonwhites helps to account for their lower fertility rate (Kiser and Frank, 1967).

Certain characteristics of housing are also closely related to the nature of the fertility differential by color. The 1960 census provided a tabulation of the number of children ever born[3] per 1,000 women 35–44 years

---

[3] *Children ever born* refers to the total number of children ever born to the mother, whether or not they are presently living.

old (married and with husband present in the home) by color, by occupation group and income of the husband, by number of housing units in the structure, and by whether or not the housing unit in which they lived had all of a given list of characteristics. These were: "direct access, kitchen or cooking equipment, sound or deteriorating condition, flush toilet and bath for exclusive use, hot piped water, and less than 1.01 persons per room." Among women in urban areas reporting all of these amenities, the average number of children born tended to be lower for nonwhites than for whites of similar status. Among women reporting that one or more of the list of amenities was lacking, the fertility rates tended to be higher for nonwhites than whites. The chief exceptions were the lower fertility for nonwhite than for white wives of men of "white-collar" occupations and living in single-family houses (U.S. Bureau of the Census, 1964).

It is of course possible that the relatively low fertility rates of nonwhite women reporting all the desirable housing characteristics results in part from selective factors. The financial and other requirements to live in modern housing may be more severe for nonwhites than whites, causing a greater selectivity of families with no or few children among nonwhites than among whites.

Thus, the 1960 census demonstrates that the percentage excess of fertility of nonwhites over whites is greatest at the youngest ages and smallest at the oldest ages of the childbearing period. Among women under twenty-five, the fertility rates of nonwhites surpasses that of whites at all socioeconomic levels. Among women twenty-five years and over, the fertility rates of nonwhites tends to fall below that of whites at high socioeconomic levels and to surpass that of whites at low and middle socioeconomic levels. Data on age at marriage of the woman indicated the critical importance of the wife's age at marriage to the direction of the differentials in fertility rate by color and socioeconomic status. Instances of lower fertility rates of nonwhites than of whites of similar socioeconomic status were much more frequent among couples with wives marrying at ages twenty-two and over. Relating fertility rates to housing characteristics indicated that instances of lower fertility of nonwhites than whites were much more frequent among couples living in houses having all of a series of modern conveniences than among those living in housing lacking one or more of the favorable housing characteristics.

Until fairly recently there was virtually no information on differences in ideals of family size and family-planning practices between white and nonwhite families. The Growth of American Families Study for 1960 provided the first such information for a nationwide sample. The purpose of this study, conducted by the Scripps Foundation for Research in Population Problems and the Survey Research Center of the University of Michigan, was to obtain information about the attitudes and behavior that determine the number of children born to married couples in the United States.[4] The basic information for the study came from interviews with a nationwide sample of wives 18–39 years of age, currently living with their husbands or with husbands temporarily absent in the Armed Forces. The respondents were chosen by area probability sampling to assure that they adequately represented all wives of the designated ages in the United States. The sample included 2,684 wives; 2,414 white and 270 nonwhite. Although the sample size is small, some of the differences between white and nonwhite couples were so great that even a small sample was large enough to reveal them. Table 1 shows the numbers of cases on which the averages and percentages presented

Table 1.   *Number of white and nonwhite couples in sample, by region of residence, southern farm residence, and wife's education, 1960.*

Characteristic	White	Nonwhite
Total	2,414	270
Region		
Northeast	581	41
North Central	715	74
South	744	136
West	374	19
Southern farm residence		
None	1,784	116
Some, not on farm now[a]	540	121
On farm now	90	33
Wife's education		
College	427	37
High school 4 years	1,153	73
High school 1–3 years	579	86
Grade school	255	74

[a]Either husband, wife, or both have lived on a farm sometime.

[4]The findings reported here are based on research carried out while the author, Dr. Arthur A. Campbell, was at the Scripps Foundation, Miami University, Oxford, Ohio, and do not necessarily represent the views of the U.S. Public Health Service.

here are based. Most of the nonwhite wives were Negro (256). In addition there were ten Japanese, one Chinese, one American Indian, one Eskimo, and one native of Guam.

PAST, EXPECTED, AND DESIRED
NUMBER OF CHILDREN

When asked how many children they would have if they could have just the number they wanted and then stop, nonwhite wives gave replies that averaged 2.9 children and white wives gave replies that averaged 3.3. Even with limitations of small sample size and our imperfect measure of the number of children wanted, it is clear that the *desired* fertility goals of nonwhite married women were lower than those of white married women.

In spite of their wishes, nonwhite wives in the sample have had and expect to have more births than white wives. The averages in Table 2 show that the past fertility rate of nonwhite wives exceeded that of white wives by 17% (2.7 births by 1960 versus 2.3).[5] The relative difference between the total births expected by nonwhite and white wives was proportional (16%) to the difference in births already experienced by each group (3.6 for nonwhite wives and 3.1 for white wives).

The data in Table 2 show that the widest differences in fertility rates between white and nonwhite couples are found in the South, especially the rural South, and among couples with little education. While there are only 33 nonwhite rural southern wives in the sample, their average of 4.5 births by time of interview is significantly higher than the average of 2.1 for white wives living on farms in the South.[6] The nonwhite wives in this group had not only borne over twice as many children as comparable white wives but expected over twice as many altogether (5.9 versus 2.9).

As Negroes move from southern rural areas to towns and cities, their fertility rate is greatly modified. Nonwhite couples with previous southern farm residence (that is, either husband or wife, or both, had lived on a southern farm at some time) had an average of 2.6 births and expected 3.5 altogether (Table 2). While these figures are well below

---

[5]Note that the differentials shown here relate to currently married women living with their husband; the data cited earlier was for ever-married women.

[6]The differential cited here between rural nonwhite and rural white wives is consistent with census data. Relevant comparisons are shown in Whelpton, Campbell, and Patterson, 1966, pp. 339 and 340.

Table 2. *Average number of births by 1960 and of most likely expected total births, and average number of children wife wants, for white and nonwhite wives, by region of residence, southern farm residence, and education, 1960.*

Characteristic	Births by 1960		Most likely expected total births		Total children wanted	
	White	Non-white	White	Non-white	White	Non-white
Total	2.3	2.7	3.1	3.6	3.3	2.9
Region						
Northeast	2.4	2.3	3.2	2.9	3.5	2.5
North Central	2.4	2.2	3.3	3.4	3.4	2.8
South	2.1	3.2	2.9	4.0	3.0	3.0
West	2.4	a	3.2	a	3.3	a
Southern farm residence						
None	2.3	2.4	3.2	3.1	3.4	2.6
Some, not on farm now[b]	1.9	2.6	2.9	3.5	3.1	2.9
On farm now	2.1	4.5	2.9	5.9	3.1	3.8
Wife's education						
College	2.0	1.7	3.0	2.4	3.3	2.4
High school 4 years	2.1	1.9	3.0	2.9	3.2	2.7
High school 1–3 years	2.6	3.0	3.3	3.8	3.3	2.7
Grade school	3.1	3.9	3.7	4.7	3.5	3.5

[a]Average not computed because there are fewer than 20 cases in base.
[b]Either husband, wife, or both have lived on a farm sometime.

the corresponding ones for couples still living on southern farms, they are still above those for nonwhites with no southern farm background, suggesting that previous southern farm residence has some influence on the fertility rate of nonwhite married couples. In the present sample, nearly half (45%) of the nonwhite wives reported that they or their husbands had lived on a southern farm at some time in their lives, and it would seem reasonable to assume that the influence of southern rural ways of life is still widespread in the nonwhite population.

When we come to nonwhite couples with *no* previous southern farm residence, we find that average past and expected numbers of births do not differ significantly from those of white couples. In other words, by the time nonwhite couples are one generation or more removed from the rural South, their fertility rate is very much like that of the white population (see Table 2). The proportion of couples with no rural southern background should rise greatly in another generation, and the influence of southern rural patterns of fertility behavior will inevitably diminish.

Educational attainment is also closely related to white-nonwhite fertility differences. The excess of nonwhite over white fertility is greatest among the least-educated wives (Table 2). Among wives with only a grade school education, nonwhites have had and expect about 25% more births than whites. At the upper end of the educational continuum, however, nonwhite wives with a college education have had and expect *fewer* births than white wives in the same educational category. What we see in these differentials is the gradual adoption of attitudes and practices favoring small families as Negroes move from farms to cities and as their educational attainment rises. The culmination of this process is a well-educated Negro upper class with relatively few children.[7]

If we combine relatively well-educated nonwhite couples (the wife has finished high school or has had some college education) and those nonwhite couples with less education but who have never lived on a southern farm, we find that the past and expected fertility of this combined group is nearly the same as for white married couples. Nonwhite wives in this group expect an average of 3.0 births, as compared with 3.1 for white wives. The average numbers of births by 1960 are 2.2 for nonwhites and 2.3 for whites.[8] Inasmuch as this broad group, members of which are defined either by relatively high education or by lack of southern farm background, contains 63% of the nonwhite sample, we may say that a majority of nonwhite married couples have and expect about the same number of children as white couples in similarly defined socioeconomic groups.

The most important facts brought out here are that (1) nonwhite wives do not want more children than white wives, and probably want fewer; (2) that the fertility rate of a majority of nonwhite wives does not differ widely from that of white wives in similarly defined groups; and (3) that the differences that exist for the remainder of the nonwhite married couples are closely associated with characteristics that will have less influence in the future than they do now—previous and current southern farm residence and low educational attainment. These findings give us some basis for expecting that fertility differences between whites and nonwhites will become narrower (see Lee and Lee, 1959).

---

[7]For a discussion of the low-fertility patterns of upper-class nonwhite couples, see Frazier, 1949, pp. 331–332.

[8]The averages presented here cannot be reconstructed from the tables given, but rather are based on data used to prepare Table 186 in Whelpton, Campbell, and Patterson, 1966, p. 345.

FECUNDITY

There is reason to believe that in the recent past impairments of the reproductive system were more common among nonwhites than whites. One item of evidence is the high proportion of older nonwhite women who are childless. The 1960 census shows that among ever-married women 50–54 years old, for example, the proportion who never had any children was 28% for nonwhites and 20% for whites. It seems likely that most of the childlessness among nonwhites was involuntary (due to physiological impairments), while most of that among whites was due to the voluntary prevention of pregnancy (Kiser, 1959).

The 1960 census also shows that the percentage of ever-married women who are childless has declined to 14% for nonwhite women 25–29 years old and to 12% for white women of similar age. In other words, if we use the prevalence of childlessness as a rough indicator of the presence of fecundity impairments, it appears that young nonwhite wives are more fecund than nonwhite wives a generation earlier and are now about as fecund as young white wives.

Data from the present study show no substantial white-nonwhite differences in the prevalence of fecundity impairments. The proportions Subfecund[9] are 33% for nonwhites and 31% for whites. Although the overall proportions with impaired fecundity are about the same for whites and nonwhites, there do appear to be some minor differences in the kinds of impairments. Some 6% of white wives reported that they or their husbands had undergone an operation for the purpose of preventing conception, while only 3% of nonwhites wives reported such operations. However, nonwhites and whites are similar in the proportion of wives (4%) reporting operations that prevent pregnancy, but that were performed to correct a pathological condition.

FAMILY PLANNING

The use of family-planning methods is less common among nonwhite than among white married couples. By the time of interview, 59% of the nonwhite couples had practiced family planning as compared with 81% of the white couples. The percentages who had used or expected to

---

[9]This word is capitalized because it was used in a special sense in this study. Couples were classified as Subfecund if there was any reason to suspect that they were below normal in their ability to have children. For the more precise definition, see Whelpton, Campbell, and Patterson, 1966, Chapter 4.

use planning methods were somewhat closer: 76% for nonwhites and 87% for whites. However, the differences are statistically significant.

The use of family planning among nonwhites is also closely related to southern farm residence. Only 36% of the nonwhite wives living on southern farms reported that they or their husbands had tried to limit family size (Table 3). This is the lowest proportion found for any socio-economic group in this study. Another 15% of southern farm residents expected to limit family size, so that slightly over half of them (some 52%) had either used planning methods or expected to do so. Of the 48% who expected never to use them, 27% were Subfecund and probably most of them would not need to prevent additional pregnancies. Thus, 21% were fecund (normal in their ability to have children) and did not expect to ever try to limit family size.

Of nonwhite couples who have lived on a southern farm, but no longer do so, some 60% have used family planning methods. Apparently

Table 3. *Percentages of couples who have used or expect to use contraception, for white and nonwhite couples, by region or residence, southern farm residence, and wife's education, 1960.*

Characteristic	Have used contraception		Have used or expect to use contraception		Do not expect to use contraception	
	White	Non-white	White	Non-white	White	Non-white
Total	81	59	87	76	13	24
Region						
Northeast	77	76	85	95	15	5
North Central	82	59	88	76	12	24
South	83	51	88	68	12	32
West	80	a	89	a	11	a
Southern farm residence						
None	81	65	83	78	12	22
Some, not on farm now[b]	80	60	86	80	14	20
On farm now	86	36	87	52	13	48
Wife's education						
College	88	86	93	95	7	5
High school 4 years	83	67	90	81	10	19
High school 1–3 years	78	56	85	79	15	21
Grade School	66	42	72	57	28	43

[a]Average not computed because there are fewer than 20 cases in base.
[b]Either husband, wife, or both have lived on a farm sometime.

the move from rural to urban areas does much to change attitudes toward family size and the use of planning methods to prevent pregnancies. Another possibility is that migration is a selective process in that the men and women who leave the farms are already more ambitious and more likely to want to plan their families than those who stay. Also, we must remember that some of the husbands and wives with southern rural backgrounds left those areas when they were children and have grown up among people who knew about and used family planning methods. The proportion who expect to use such methods (80%) is not far from the proportion for whites with similar rural southern backgrounds (86%).

Nonwhite wives with a college education report a high prevalence of use. Altogether, 95% of them have used or expect to use planning methods as compared with 93% for college-educated whites (Table 3). Again, it appears that better-educated nonwhite couples readily adopt moderate family-size goals and methods of attaining them. This suggests that continued improvements in the education of nonwhites will bring an increase in the proportion using family planning.

FERTILITY PLANNING

Nonwhite couples have been much less successful than whites in planning fertility. However, the two groups differ most sharply at the two extremes—Completely Planned Fertility and Excess Fertility[10]—and we shall focus attention mainly on the proportions in these groups. Only 7% of the nonwhite couples have achieved Completely Planned Fertility, compared with 21% for whites (Table 4). However, the most important contrast is in the Excess Fertility category: 31% for nonwhites and 17% for whites.

As might be expected from previously described differentials, the white-nonwhite differences in planning status are greatest among cou-

---

[10]The planning status groups are defined as follows:

Completely Planned: Users with no pregnancies and other users who stopped using contraception before every pregnancy in order to conceive.

Partly Planned: Couples who had one or more conceptions before starting to use contraception because they wanted these conceptions as soon as possible. Any conception after use began occurred when contraception was stopped in order to conceive.

Partly Unplanned: Couples who have had one or more "unplanned" pregnancies, but have not had more pregnancies than wanted.

Excess Fertility: Either the husband or the wife or both did not want another child at the time of the last conception.

ples on farms in the South. Among nonwhites living on southern farms, nearly half (48%) have had more pregnancies than the husband or wife wanted. This is the highest prevalence of Excess Fertility found for any socioeconomic group in the study. It compares with 20% for white couples on southern farms. The only white group with a level of Excess Fertility anywhere near that of the nonwhite farm population consists of those of low education (wife did not go beyond grade school) and a low income (husband's salary less than $4,000 a year). Of such couples, 39% reported Excess Fertility.

Nonwhite couples who left the rural South are more successful family planners than those who remain, but they are still not so successful as whites. About 8% of this group have Completely Planned Fertility as compared with 22% among similar whites. About 29% of nonwhites no longer living on southern farms report Excess Fertility, still well above the 18% reported for whites. Obviously the move from the southern farm to other areas has brought with it a substantial improvement in

Table 4. *Percentage of couples with completely planned or excess fertility, for white and nonwhite couples, by region of residence, southern farm residence, and wife's education, 1960.*

Characteristic	Completely planned fertility		Excess fertility	
	White	Nonwhite	White	Nonwhite
Total	21	7	17	31
Region				
Northeast	19	7	14	24
North Central	22	12	17	23
South	25	4	18	38
West	16	a	21	a
Southern farm residence				
None	21	9	17	28
Some, not on farm now[b]	22	7	18	29
On farm now	27	—	20	48
Wife's education				
College	35	24	11	19
High school 4 years	24	7	14	16
High school 1–3 years	13	5	21	38
Grade school	6	1	32	43

[a]Average not computed because there are fewer than 20 cases in base.
[b]Either husband, wife, or both have lived on a farm sometime.

the success with which nonwhite couples plan their families; but they still have not achieved the levels observed for the white population.

The extent to which nonwhites differ from whites in their family-planning practices can also be seen when we compare the different education groups (Table 4). In every educational category, including the college group, nonwhite couples have shown less success in family planning than white couples; their level of Completely Planned Fertility is lower, and their level of Excess Fertility is higher.

Apparently, planning status is one fertility variable in which non-whites differ consistently from whites, regardless of socioeconomic status. The white-nonwhite differentials vary in magnitude, but the nonwhite value is greater in all educational groups and all regions of the country (Table 4).

SUMMARY

The rapid cultural change that the nonwhite population is undergoing has left its mark on fertility differences between whites and nonwhites. We find that nonwhite couples have had and expect more births than white couples and that this difference is brought about partly by the unusually high fertility of a minority of nonwhite couples who live in the rural South, and partly by the moderately high fertility of the many nonwhite couples who have southern farm origins. Nonwhite couples with no southern farm background have and expect about the same number of births as similar white couples. These differentials suggest that as the influence of southern rural patterns of mating and child-bearing diminishes, the fertility differences between whites and non-whites will decline.

It is clear that nonwhite wives do not want as many children as they expect to have. They want about the same number as white wives or fewer.

Although there is some evidence that in the past there was a greater prevalence of fecundity impairments in the nonwhite population, the present study gives us no reason to believe that this is still true.

A lower proportion of nonwhites than of whites have used family planning methods and a lower proportion expect to have done so by the end of the childbearing period. Even among couples using planning methods, nonwhite couples are considerably less successful in controlling fertility than white couples. This seems to be true in all socio-economic groups.

REFERENCES

Frazier, F. E. 1949. *The Negro in the United States.* New York: Macmillan.

Kiser, C. V. 1959. Fertility trends and differentials among nonwhites in the United States. *Milbank Memorial Fund Quarterly* 36: 149–197.

Kiser, C. V., and M. E. Frank. 1967. Factors associated with the low fertility of nonwhite women of college education. *Milbank Memorial Fund Quarterly* 45: 43–59.

Kiser, C. V., W. H. Grabill, and A. A. Campbell. 1968. *Trends and variations in fertility in the United States.* Cambridge, Mass.: Harvard Univ. Press.

Lee, A., and E. Lee. 1959. The future fertility of the American Negro. *Social Forces* 37: 228–231.

U.S. Bureau of the Census. 1964. *Women by number of children ever born. 1960 census of population. PC(2)-3A. Tables 25 and 44.* Washington, D.C.: Government Printing Office.

Whelpton, P. K., A. A. Campbell, and J. E. Patterson. 1966. *Fertility and family planning in the United States.* Princeton, N.J.: Princeton Univ. Press.

In modern societies it is the social environment rather than the physical environment that determines which members of the population will increase or decline. Public health measures and medical services have lowered death rates for all segments of society. However, where there is poverty and where standards of education are low, the birth rate stays high. To deprive any part of the population of employment opportunities and high education is to foster that group's increase in a continuing cycle of poverty and low education.

Races and the Future of Man

FREDERICK OSBORN
The Population Council
New York, New York

No one knows what capacities, physical, intellectual, or emotional, may be needed to fill all the niches in our complex and changing civilization. Ask any dozen people and they might describe a number of ideal types, but probably give little thought to the environment these perfect men would have to function in. This would certainly be putting the cart before the horse. Nature did not work that way. In the long time during the first living cells evolved into the complexity of man, nature was simply selecting the various stocks that survived from one generation to another. Man survived in many different environments, and both physical qualities and intelligence were factors in his survival.

With the coming of a more civilized life, the relationship between physical characteristics and survival became less direct. Social and psychological factors began to influence size of family. The risk of death was affected more by occupation than by personal characteristics. We do not know what was the course of evolution during this recent period, but there is no evidence that, on the whole today, human stocks are either superior or inferior in their genetic make-up to the people of ten thousand years ago. What has been added has been a social structure so complex that man's capacity to handle it is stretched to the limit. If man's genetic constitution should now deteriorate, his future would be dark indeed.

Today in the United States over 97% of all children born alive live to be 30 or more. Death is no longer selective with respect to differences in intelligence or personality. In a eugenically oriented society, selection for these qualities must be effected by differences in size of family between people of different kinds of intelligence and different personal qualities. In general, it appears that, with the exception of certain sterility problems, differences in size of family are not much influenced by differences in health or other personal characteristics, but result mainly from a great variety of economic, social, and psychological pressures which influence married people in deciding how many children they will have.

The interest of eugenics is in how these influences affect the decisions of different types of couples as to the size of their families. Under what circumstances do intelligent people have more children than the less intelligent? Are the reactions of racial minority groups different from those of the white majority? Should people belonging to minority races be treated as a group, or on an individual basis? Are the public's views on race based on the facts? To answer these questions we must first ask, what is race, and how do the races differ in socially significant attributes.

At the end of the nineteenth century the idea that there was a hierarchy of races was widely accepted by many in the upper classes of Europe and Great Britain. After the *liberté* and *egalité* of the French Revolution, it was comfortable for the well-to-do to feel that they belonged to a superior race, with their position justified and secured by nature.

Early in this century the new science of human genetics made it suddenly and abundantly clear that biological inheritance is not a blend of the qualities of the father and mother, but a recombination of the thousands of their genes passed on by inheritance. Each gene contributes to specific characteristics and is passed on separately in its individual entirety. A particular gene may be passed on through the mother, another through the father, and this is as true of the genes that contribute to the development of intelligence and personality as it is of those that determine eye color.

Except for identical twins, no two individuals have the same set of genes. That two people have the same genes for skin color does not mean that they have the same genes for blood group or intelligence, or for any other quality. People called of one race because they have the same color and physical proportions are found to differ among each other in almost every other characteristic.

Human beings have a deep emotional interest in their own kind. We tend to distrust people who are different in features, color, or behavior. Huck Finn and Jim, the runaway slave, had a long discussion as to whether the two Frenchmen were people. It was decided that they were not, since Huck and Jim could neither understand them nor be understood. Any of us, however generous our natures, who have ever associated with people entirely lacking in education, or with people stricken by poverty or by disease, must admit, I think, that our pity is not unmixed with a sense of superiority. If the human spirit is thus so protective of self, we must approach the scientific findings on race with a detachment and objectivity that may tax our powers.

SCIENTIFIC FINDINGS ON RACE

The first classifications of the races of man were made from visual observations of color and physical form. By the nineteenth century these were being supplemented by more careful measurements of physical characteristics and pigmentation. Scientists reached general agreement on a broad division of most men into three main groups or races: Mongoloid, Negroid, and Caucasoid. Theories were evolved to account for racial differences. Some held that inheritance was by "blood," and that a mixture of bloods "diluted" the strain, which was then no longer "pure." With the turn of the twentieth century, theories about race began to be tested against scientific facts developed by anthropologists in the field and by the new sciences of genetics and psychology. Today, there is general agreement among scientists on a number of findings about race, some in rather startling contrast to earlier theories.

The elaboration of these findings is beyond the scope of this article or the competence of its author. For their significance to the progress of eugenics, we need only list and briefly summarize those particularly related to our subject.

Differences within races are greater than average differences between races for many important characteristics. The major races, and the sub-groups into which they are sometimes broken down, are not composed of individuals all of whom are alike. Except for general similarities in color and form of face and body, which are their so-called racial characteristics, individuals may and generally do differ widely, even in their physical characteristics, while showing every sort of variation in intelligence and personal qualities. And on the borders of every race there are individuals whose particular assignment is doubtful.

There is no scientific evidence for "superior races." Over the long past the physical differences between the races must have borne some relation to the various environments in which the differentiation took place. But today it is hard to prove that the differences are suited to particular environments, except in the case of some specialized group like the Eskimo or the differences between white and Negro in adaptation to moist heat and cold. All races produce individuals differing widely in vitality, longevity, athletic ability, and endurance, with almost no measurable differences in the average between different races. In intelligence and personal traits, whose development is greatly affected by even small differences in the environment, the average differences are no greater than can be accounted for by known differences in the environment.

Studies in human genetics indicate no "pure" races. Genes for various important characteristics are found in different frequencies in populations all over the world. The genes that determine the inheritance of blood groups and blood *antigens* furnish an excellent example of the diversity within each race. The different blood groups are inherited as separate entities. The genes for the four best known groups, A, B, AB, and O, are widely scattered through all the major races. Yet type A is dangerously antipathetic to type B, and vice-versa. A white man of type A will be killed by a transfusion of B blood from another white man, but benefit just as much by a transfusion of A blood from a Negro as from another white man with A blood.

Of the major races, none is more "primitive" than another. "Primitive" characteristics are about equally scattered among the major racial groups. The thin lips of the white for instance, are simian, compared with the full nonsimian lips of the Negro. But the Negro has a flat broad more simian nose, compared to the thin nonsimian nose of the white. The list of such comparisons can be extended almost indefinitely. They show differences between races, but do not give evidence of evolutionary "superiority."

Hereditary defect and susceptibility to disease. Genetic defects are the results of mutations, and races do not differ in the rules that govern the distribution of mutations. A high incidence of defect in small isolated communities cannot be assigned to race, but to conditions that have brought about and maintained a high concentration of defect in a particular locality.

The controversy on "racial intelligence." When people speak of one race being "more intelligent" than another, they are usually implying that the differences in intelligence are due to a difference in the genetic or hereditary quality of the different races. They are thinking of a sort of "racial intelligence," as though intelligence was the product of some inner force. But intelligence develops only in reaction to an environment. A child kept from all human contacts grows up wholly disoriented and unable to take any intelligent part. Given superior educational environments, children average better intelligence than do their friends with less education. There are differences in the hereditary capacity for developing intelligence, but in the process of development, heredity and environment are almost inextricably intertwined.

Identical twins have exactly the same heredity. By studying identical twins separated in early infancy and given different kinds of homes and different amounts of education, we find that test intelligence is directly related to extent of education, and the twins may differ to a marked extent if their education has been different. But in a closely similar educational environment the tested intelligence of identical twins is usually extraordinarily alike, while nontwin brothers in the same environment may show marked differences in test intelligence. Such studies give evidence that individuals differ in genetic capacity for intelligence, but give almost no information on whether the genetic differences or the environmental differences or a combination of both are responsible for the differences between any particular two individuals.

Races are composed of great numbers of individuals, each differing from the next in genetic capacities and in the environment in which he has grown up. To measure all these individual differences and then get an average genetic capacity for a race as a whole would, of course, be an impossible task. The very nature of intelligence tests makes them of little value for racial comparisons, because a test developed on one race may not touch the experience of another. You can't test the intelligence of a farm boy by asking him the cost of a ride on the subway, or that of a city boy by asking him which end of a cow gets up first.

Only one conclusion is possible from the studies which have been made to date. Differences in test intelligence between the major races are no greater than can be accounted for by the known differences in their environments. On this there is general scientific agreement.

Race mixture. Both inbreeding within small isolated groups and outbreeding or race mixture have been essential factors in the evolution of man. From the earliest times in human history, migrations, wars, and even sometimes tribal customs have promoted the mixture of different populations. Recombination of hereditary variations derived from many different ancestral stocks is a major factor in the physical variety of individuals within every race.

THE EUGENIC ASPECTS

Changes in human characteristics can take place rapidly. The evolution of man took a long time. But as he became established in all his variety, changes in the proportion of the different varieties could take place rapidly. Whenever the environment changed in such a way as to help or to hinder the survival of an existing characteristic, then the proportion of people with that characteristic could be changed in only a few generations. The introduction of birth control is an example of how rapidly new conditions can make themselves felt.

The first result of the introduction of birth control in the United States was a reduction of births among the more educated people, with no corresponding reduction among the poorer and less educated. The differential between these groups reached its peak during the 1930s. In a 1935 study of a national sample of white women, the variations in general fertility for the average of 100 were 69 for college women, 95 for high school women, 125 for seventh-to-eighth-grade graduates, and 146 for those who left school before the seventh grade (Kiser, 1942). Many social scientists were concerned by such differentials in births. Whatever their genetic effect, they were a handicap to education and social advance. Since World War II there has been a leveling off of these differentials in the white population, with little change among nonwhites. In 1960 a national sample of white and nonwhite married women, ages 18-39, was interviewed. While these women had not yet quite completed their childbearing, it was possible to predict fairly accurately the final size of family to be expected at different educational levels of the wife. Variations in size of family by education were as shown in Table 1.

Since the educational levels of children tend on the whole to follow the level of the parents, the differentials in the whole population in 1935 must have been a serious handicap to educational advances. By 1960 the differentials among white people were largely reversed from that of the whole population of twenty years ago, but the nonwhite population still showed the old differentials, and to that extent they are handicapped in their efforts to improve the education of their children.

With today's public health and medical services, the death rate everywhere is low; but where there is poverty and where standards of education are poor, the birth rate stays high. Among Negroes in the past, death rates were high and birth rates were reduced by sterility. Thus, (without allowance for immigration) the proportion of Negroes declined from 19.1% of the total population in 1790 to 14.1% in 1860;

Table 1. *Average number of births expected among women 18–39, by wife's education, 1960.*

Education	Nonwhite	White
College	2.4	3.0
High school 4 years	2.9	3.0
High school 1–3 years	3.8	3.3
Grade school	4.7	3.7
Total	3.6	3.1

Source. Unpublished material, second Growth of American Families Study, 1960, letter from Arthur A. Campbell to author, 6/11/63.

11.6% in 1900, and to a low of 9.7% in 1930; it rose to 10.6% in 1960 and is still rising. Net rates of reproduction for 1905–1910 were whites, 1,339 and nonwhites, 1,329; for 1935, whites, 958 and nonwhites, 1,108; for 1956, whites, 1,660 and nonwhites, 2,178; and for 1960, whites, 1,664 and nonwhites, 2,093. Even more important, Negro families with a better education are now having smaller families than the corresponding whites, while low socioeconomic-group Negroes have more children than the corresponding whites.

This would be a dangerous trend if it should continue for long. The least educated parents have in turn the least educated children, and our efforts towards a higher level of education can be largely or wholly offset by such differentials in births.

Every racial group possesses all of the different genes which condition or impart the differing capacities to respond or adapt to the good and bad environments of our complex society. The frequency of these different genes will increase or decrease according to the reproductive rates of individuals across this full range of environments. The lesson of the last thirty years is that those individuals, whatever their racial group, who have a good education, good economic conditions, and access to effective methods of birth control will have a relatively low birth rate; while those individuals who have a poor education, poor economic conditions, and limited access to birth control will have a high birth rate. This means that any genes which increase adaptation to a good environment will decrease and those more compatible with a poor environment will increase. This is the kind of dysgenic situation that eugenics seeks to remedy.

THE ROAD TO EUGENIC IMPROVEMENT

Eugenics is not concerned with color of skin or facial or bodily characteristics, unless it is shown that these features of man are related to his genetic capacity for socially valuable qualities, such as intelligence and character. Such a relationship has never been proved and theoretically is highly improbable.

Eugenics is not much concerned with the unsolved question of whether the proportion of hereditary ability is greater in one race than in another. Eugenics is concerned with saving the genes for superior ability wherever they are found and increasing their frequency. It would do this by a return to a process of selection, different in method but similar in results to the selection practiced in nature in the past, and just as unconscious. Since the death rate is everywhere uniformly low, and deaths are no longer selective for ability, selection must be by variations in birth rates. The voluntary decisions of parents as to size of family, made in their own interests, must be on the whole of a sort to favor the interests of society in the improvement of the next generation. To further such a process of selection, the social environment must meet the following conditions:

A. An adequate education for all. (Where there is little education, there is a high birth rate.)

B. Effective birth control available to all. (Where effective birth control methods are not made available, there is a high birth rate.)

C. An easy road to selective job placement. (Unless individuals find jobs for which they are naturally fitted, there can be no selection for diverse abilities.)

For a good many years we have been moving toward a form of society which meets these conditions for the white population. The results are evident in the trend to a reversal of educational and socioeconomic birth differentials which has been taking place among white people since World War II; that is, individuals in the higher socioeconomic groups are having as many or more children as those in low socioeconomic groups, in contrast to the period before the war. But we have moved slowly, if at all, to meet these conditions in our Negro population. The Negro does not receive an adequate education; he is not provided birth control services; he is kept out of a variety of jobs even when he is obviously fitted for them; and finally the balance of social pressures is such that the Negro couples of the higher socioeconomic groups find less reason to have large families than do the corresponding whites. As a result, the Negro population, while increasing faster than the white, is showing socioeconomic birth differentials which are still dysgenic, as they were among whites twenty-five and more years ago.

Eugenics requires that the conditions necessary for a eugenically effective form of society be met for all people and races in the American melting pot. We cannot afford for long to countenance environments in which job opportunities and education are not equally available, in which subservience is necessary for survival, or staying on relief is the only means of supporting one's children.

REFERENCES

Kiser, Clyde V. 1942. *Group Differences in urban fertility.* Baltimore: Williams and Wilkins.

U.S. Bureau of the Census. *Census of population, 1960. Final Report P. C. (1)-1B.* Washington, D.C.

U.S. Bureau of the Census. 1960. *Historical statistics of the United States, colonial times to 1957.* Washington, D.C.

The History and Nature of Race Classification

RICHARD H. OSBORNE
*Department of Biobehavorial Sciences**
University of Connecticut
Storrs, Connecticut

Racism and race classification are often erroneously equated. Each had its independent origin, despite the fact that the two have become interrelated at times through the course of historical events. Some form of racism has doubtless existed from the very earliest days of human social organization when diverse peoples came into contact, and was based then as now upon the fear and mistrust engendered by physical and cultural differences. Race classification, on the other hand, had its beginnings in scientific inquiry, originating and continuing in serious pursuit of a systematic body of knowledge about man.

The idea of making objective and systematic classifications of natural phenomena such as plants and animals—and man himself—had its beginnings in the sixteenth century with the new philosophy of scientific observation and inductive reasoning under the principles formulated by Francis Bacon. Before that time, few classificatory systems existed for any natural phenomena. In general, man saw the world around him in about as subjective a manner as Augustine in the third century who classified animals into three major groupings—"helpful, hurtful, and superfluous." After Bacon, the far-reaching explorations of the next two centuries—from the South Pacific islands to the Arctic tundra—meant the discovery of a vast variety of plants and animals. Samples and descriptions of these were brought back to Europe, providing a wealth of material to be examined in a "scientific" manner.

The man responsible for bringing order to these studies of the plant and animal world was Carl Linnaeus, a Swedish botanist, who in his

---
*Written while on leave from the University of Wisconsin as Research Professor at the University of Connecticut.

great work *Systema Natura* devised a hierarchical classificatory system for plants (1735) and later for animals (1758), so that any individual specimen could be identified by specific features and placed with related forms within a particular category of the system. A certain number of categories at one level that had some important characteristic in common could then all fit within the next larger category and so on, culminating in the widest of the categories, the kingdoms.

In the Linnaean, as in any other classificatory system, the number of levels or types of groupings is arbitrary. To a great extent they represent the degree of the classifier's awareness of important similarities or differences in those items he is classifying and at any given moment reflect the scientific knowledge of the day. For example, until Linnaeus created the term for "mammals," there had been no word in any of the European languages to describe specifically those animals that have hair and suckle their young. The English word "beast" was the closest equivalent, but it could also be applied to large reptiles. It took a special insight to see those common characteristics that make mammals a well-delineated "natural" group.

In many ways, it is a succession of insights that scientists have passed through in studying man as part of the animal world. As a result, man's place within the zoological classificatory system has changed with time —as has the system itself—sometimes reflecting a new concept, such as that of *evolution*[1] in the nineteenth century, sometimes reflecting new data gained by technological advances. Reclassifications have been common throughout the system as a whole, and even the placement of certain organisms in the proper kingdom had to await modern scientific knowledge and technology.

The present zoological classification of man is given in Table A1. The systematic hierarchy of classification that has now been developed reflects, as far as possible, the probable evolutionary sequence of living organisms. This modification of the Linnaean system followed from Darwin's formulations of 1859 and from other changes that have taken place since 1900 as a consequence of the development of the science of genetics. While these two events did not appreciably change the Linnaean system, they did bring about fundamental changes in how the system is applied. For example, while the only real unit in nature is the individual organism, the individual cannot be "classified," only identified as deriving from a certain population (Simpson, 1962). Only populations have continuity through time and can therefore be classified within

---

[1]Words defined in the Glossary (p. 173) are italicized the first time they appear in each paper.

an evolutionary scheme. In this context, the basic unit is the species, the genetically closed system within which populations exist. However, until the genetic nature of a species was recognized and fully accepted, which was not until the 1930s and 1940s, classification at the species level was arbitrary. In fact, there was even considerable confusion over the theoretical basis of the system itself.

The new genetic definition of a species can be given as "groups of actually or potentially interbreeding natural populations, which are reproductively (genetically) isolated from other such groups" (Simpson, 1962). However, we cannot apply this definition to extinct populations of organisms of which we have only fossil remains. Thus, we also need an "evolutionary" definition of a species. Viewing sequential populations through time, we see the species as a lineage or ancestral-descendent sequence of populations evolving from others and with its own unitary evolutionary role and tendencies (Simpson, 1962). The species then is the basic unit of evolution.

These new concepts of the species have had an important influence on the concept of race. But before we can even talk about racial classifications, we must consider a level of differences that falls below that of species differences. The lowest category generally recognized in the formal zoological classification is that of the subspecies. These are not genetically closed units, as are species, but represent distinct breeding populations within a species which have been reproductively isolated one from the other for a sufficient period of time to have developed a degree of genetic divergence which renders them distinguishable. Perhaps the most commonly applied criterion for subspecies differences is Amadon's rule (Amadon, 1949), which is that the differences should be such as to make it possible to distinguish accurately 75% of the individuals in each of the separate populations (see Table A1).

In general, race differences are taken to be less than subspecies differences (i.e., they would not necessarily satisfy Amadon's rule) although the terms are sometimes used interchangeably (Coon, 1965). One widely accepted criterion for defining races is that they are breeding populations that differ in the frequency of one or more genetic variants. Again, this means that we are examining a population as a whole and comparing the pattern of *gene frequencies* of that entire population with another population. Most important is the fact that subspecies and races, unlike species, are not closed genetic or evolutionary units, but simply breeding populations within which a significant number of individuals carry a particular variant of a gene common to the species. What is taken as a meaningful "racial" differentiation within any given species will depend entirely upon the classifier, the circumstances, and

Table A1. *Zoological classification of man.*

Kingdom Animalia
(Amoebae to mammals)

Members of the kingdom Animalia, one of the 4 kingdoms into which all living things are divided, are characterized by: the power of movement; consumption of other organisms rather than manufacture of their own food; a limited growth period.

Phylum Chordata
(Notachord-bearing animals)

Members of the phylum Chordata, one of the 22 phyla within Animalia, are characterized by: segmented bodies; complete digestive systems; closed blood systems; skeletons inside bodies.

Class Mammalia
(Egg-laying mammals, marsupials, and placental mammals)

Members of the class Mammalia, one of the 8 classes within Chordata, are characterized by: body hair; mammary glands; four-chambered hearts; constant body temperature; possession of nails, claws, or hoofs.

Subclass Eutheria
(Placental mammals)

Members of the subclass Eutheria, one of the 3 subclasses within Mammalia, are characterized by: allantoic placentas; shoulder girdles; one vagina; no cloaca. Most have three molar teeth on each side.

Order Primates
(Lemurs, tarsieus, monkeys, and man)

Members of the order Primates, one of the 17 orders within Eutheria, are characterized by: forward orbits which give stereoscopic vision; convoluted brains with large cerebral hemispheres; five digits on each foot; grasping feet and/or hands; opposable thumbs; a single pair of mammary glands.

Suborder Anthropoidea
(Monkeys, apes, man)

Members of the suborder Anthropoidea, one of the 2 suborders within primates, are characterized by: largely diurnal rather than nocturnal habits; being more generalized and not entirely arboreal.

Superfamily Hominoidea
(Apes and man)

Members of the superfamily Hominoidea, one of the 3 superfamilies within Anthropoidea, are characterized by: diurnal habits; being more generalized, larger, and more terrestrial than the other Anthropoidea. All are tailless.

Family Hominidae
(Living man and his more direct antecedents)

Man belongs to the family Hominidae, one of the 2 families within Hominoidea, which probably separated from the other family, Pongidae (the great apes), twenty million years ago, the equivalent of one million human generations. The family Hominidae is characterized by: large brains with greater development of frontal lobes than the great apes; rotation of the foramen magnum; small supra-orbital ridges; marked reduction of the facial skeleton; a relatively simple pattern of the molar teeth and reduction of canines; an upright posture; increased length of lower limb relative to trunk and upper limb; completely opposable thumbs and unopposable big toes.

Genus *Homo*
(Living man and his ancestors for at least the past 500,000 and possibly as long as 1,500,000 years, or 25,000 to 75,000 human generations)

There is no agreement about the number of genera within the family Hominidae, or about the characteristics which specifically define the genera. Cranial capacity within the genus *Homo* ranges from 900 to 2,000 cc. Members usually lack a diastema (space between canines and premolar teeth); temporal ridges never reach the midline of the skull; brow ridges are highly variable.

Species *sapiens*
(Living man and his ancestors for at least the last 200,000 years, the equivalent of 10,000 human generations)

The genus *Homo* is generally considered to consist of 3 species—*H. erectus*, *H. neanderthalensis*, and *H. sapiens*—although there is now a tendency to consider *neaderthalensis* and *sapiens* as variants of the same species. The species *sapiens* is characterized by: increased reduction of the facial skeleton, brow ridges and palate size; long bones that are straighter and more slender than those of *erectus* and *neanderthalensis*.

Subspecies (??)

Some taxonomists consider the so-called major races, which may have been in existence for about 30,000 years, or some 1,200 to 1,500 human generations, to be the equivalent of zoological subspecies. If the zoological definitions of subspecies are applied (Mayr, 1942; Amadon, 1949), Caucasoids, Negroids, and Mongoloids qualify as subspecies. Using Amadon's rule that 75% of the individuals of a geographical population will be unequivocably determinable, these three groups can be so distinguished on the basis of known blood-group systems, by surface features, or by skeletal features.

the purposes of the classification. The only limiting factor, as is inherent in the species definition, is that in order to be classified there must be a natural or breeding-population *descent group* with some distinguishing genetic variability.

If, then, the definition of "racial" differences is so dependent upon a knowledge of evolution and genetics, what were the rationales and criteria for racial classifications in the past? If we return to the time of Linnaeus, we find that in 1745 he proposed four races of living man (Europeans, Africans, Asiatics, and Amercan Indians) whose differentiation was based largely upon pigmentation and a subjective judgment of what were then thought to be each group's behavioral charcteristics. The first to use comparative anatomy in the study of different groups of people was a German physiologist, Johann Friedrich Blumenbach, who in 1781 published his classification of man on the basis of head shape. He divided man into five races (Caucasian, Negro, Mongol, Malayan, and American Indian). His classification was well received by scientists of his day, probably because it did have an "objective" physical basis, that of head shape. It avoided Linnaeus' subjective behavioral characteristics and more or less took into account the basic differences in pigmentation of "white, black, yellow, brown, and red" of common observation. The name "Caucasian" was coined by Blumenbach on the basis of a skull from the Caucasus region which he felt was typical of this "race," which included such disparate-appearing peoples as Swedes and Arabs.

Modifications of this classification and new ones proposing different races based on a variety of criteria followed. Among the better known of the racial anthropologists during the nineteenth century were Paul Broca and Joseph Deniker; the latter attempted to describe ten races in Europe alone.

Why were the early zoologists, anthropologists, and others interested in classifying groups of people into "races" at all? One of the reasons was simply to catalogue the many different "kinds" of men that actually existed. Remember that at the time Linnaeus published his classification in the mid-eighteenth century, Europe was still in the process of sorting out what was legendary, such as the unicorn, from what was scientifically verifiable. A clear example of this process is seen in the *Amoenitates Academicae* (Vol. VI, Leiden, 1764), published under the auspices of Linnaeus, which shows a drawing of four primates—an orang-utan holding a walking stick, a chimpanzee with a human head, hands, and feet, a woman with a tail a foot long, and another woman totally covered with hair. In the zoological naiveté of the day these forms represented man-like creatures whose existence had been vouched for by travelers to remote parts of the world. Thus, "scientific" descriptions of different "races" was a way of adding to man's knowledge about himself and the variety of forms in which he existed in the world.

During the more than a century between Linnaeus and Darwin, men measured and described other men and created racial categories and subcategories, which were scrambled and rearranged endlessly according to each investigator's interpretation of the meaning of the measurements and descriptions. Behind all these attempts at constructing racial categories was the implicit, and sometimes explicit, belief that, with the proper amount of data, human differences could eventually be sorted out in the pattern designed by the Divine Maker. There was something of an aura of theological dogmatism hanging over these kinds of classifications, a dogmatism which perhaps has been perpetuated to some extent to the present in the way many people regard "races" as not only somewhat rigid in nature but also somehow preordained to exist in a "pure" or original state. Nothing could be farther from the facts. There has never been such a thing as a "pure" race. Race formation and breakdown is a dynamic process, subject to constant change.

It is important to remember that the early classifiers were working in complete ignorance of what we today consider the two fundamental concepts necessary for the study of population variation—that of evolution and that of the genetic transmission of *particulate hereditary material* from generation to generation. It is seldom realized how recent these concepts actually are. It was not until fairly late in the nineteenth century, following Darwin, that the idea of man as part and parcel of an evolutionary progression over great periods of time was widely accepted in the scientific community. It was much later still before man's evolution became generally accepted outside of scientific circles, as is attested to by the Scopes Trial of the 1920s and the furor created by the fact that the concept of evolution was being taught in public schools.

After the acceptance of man's place in the scheme of evolution, "racial" differences had to be examined in a completely new light, and all the reasons for studying them were different. Instead of ascertaining the divine design, students of race differences were now asking: Which peoples showed evidence that processes of "natural *selection*" had been at work? What kinds of "*adaptation*" to their environment did different peoples show? Could fossil evidence be found of that simian ancestor that man and the great apes had in common? Were some living humans more "primitive," more like man's fossil ancestors, than others? It was within the context of these questions that "race" was studied and "race questions" were largely asked during the first two or even three decades of this century.

The physical anthropologist Ernest Hooton was perhaps the last to present a detailed classification of living races based solely upon comparative physical features and pre-genetic evolutionary formulations. He centered his classification on three primary races, using a limited number of sorting criteria. His sorting criteria were basically surface features, many of which are still found useful, particularly when used in conjunction with other criteria (Garn, 1971; Goldsby, 1971). Examples of the most useful of these for distinguishing the three primary races—Caucasoid, Mongoloid, and Negroid—are given in Table A2. These three races were divided into primary subraces and then into *morphological*

Table A2.   *Racial criteria based upon surface features.*[a]

Sorting Criteria	Caucasoid	Negroid	Mongoloid
Skin color	Light brown to white, pink, or ruddy.	Dark brown to black.	Yellow or yellow-brown.
Eye color	Never black, all lighter shades.	Dark brown to black.	Medium to dark brown.
Hair color	Rarely black, all lighter shades.	Black.	Black.
Hair form	Wavy to straight, sometimes loosely curled.	Woolly to frizzly.	Straight, coarse texture.
Nasal form	Usually high and narrow, index[b] under 70.	Usually low and broad, tip and alea thick, index[b] 85 and over.	Root very low, tip short, tip and alea medium, index[b] intermediate to Caucasoid and Negroid.
Malars (cheeks)	Small.	Variable, usually larger than Caucasoid.	Strong forward and lateral jut, usually covered with a flat pad.
Beard and body hair	Usually medium to heavy, highly variable.	Medium to sparse.	Less than Caucasoid or Negroid.
Membranous lip	Medium to thin, little eversion.	Usually thick, everted, marked lip seam.	Medium, variable.

[a] As proposed by Hooten and others, and customarily applied when race classification is based on surface features.
[b] Breadth x 100/height

types. Different levels of mixtures were also provided for in this system. Within each primary race there was allowance for composites of sub-races and residual mixed types, and then composites of the primary races, which were again subdivided. Such constructs are basically exercises in taxonomic gymnastics and go far beyond any hope for actual objectivity. Table A3 gives examples of the kinds of sorting criteria employed in classifying skeletal material into the three major races.

While this kind of a classification system remains useful for skeletal material, and in its results even agrees quite well with recent race classifications using additional sorting techniques, both the theoretical base for race classification and the questions to be posed in racial studies have now changed. While these changes are a consequence of the development of the science of genetics that began after the turn of the century, they did not begin to be felt until as recently as the 1940s. The two ideas that had the greatest impact on race classification were the genetic definition of a species and the concept that populations, rather than

Table A3.   *Racial criteria based upon skeletal features.*[a]

Sorting Criteria	Caucasoid	Negroid	Mongoloid
Skull	Greater development of brow ridges than in Negroids and Mongoloids; large mastoid processes.	Rounded forehead, long skull; prominent occipiput (back of skull).	Brow ridges poorly developed; round skull; flat occipiput with marked ridge; vault (top of the skull) often with a keel.
Face	Straight face; small jaws and prominent chin; high narrow nasal bones and well-developed nasal spine.	Prognathism (forward protrusion of upper jaw); small chin; low broad basal bridge and broad nasal aperture; long narrow palate.	Malars (cheek bones) prominent; root of nose flat and broad; nasal aperture narrow; palate short and wide; lower jaw wide.
Long bones	Thick; joints large and muscle markings prominent.	Slender; shin and forearm bones long relative to upper segments.	Not remarkable; intermediate to Caucasoid and Negroid.

[a] As proposed by Hooten and others, and customarily applied when a race classification of skeletal remains is made.

individuals, are what can be classified. With these realizations came some new questions: What is the nature of the distribution of genetic traits within and between populations that results in observed race differences? Are races episodes in the evolution of a species? Do different populations (races) differ in their disease susceptibility? Which of the observed differences between populations are genetic or environmental or due to the interaction of the two forces? Through studies of race differences, can man learn to control his many environments to meet advantageously the needs of genetically different populations in different circumstances? These and many other questions can now be put to race studies and an accumulating body of information concerning race differences.

Application of genetics and new kinds of laboratory techniques to race studies and classification systems have added important parameters. Use of the blood-group systems, for which the genetic mechanisms are both known and simple, has supplied objective criteria that can be handled statistically on the basis of gene frequencies within and between populations. Of the more recent classifications, Weiner (1948) described a classification based on the ABO and Rh blood systems resulting in six races. With the addition of the MN blood system, he expanded his classification to seven. Using the same systems, Boyd (1950) arrived at six races, including a hypothetical Early European Race, which he equated with the Basques on the basis of their unique gene frequencies. His six races were termed: (1) Early European, (2) European, (3) African, (4) Asiatic, (5) American Indian, and (6) Australian Aborigine. More recent classifications, using morphological traits as well as the blood groups and taking into account "breeding populations," expand this classification considerably. Dobzhansky (1962) decided upon 34 definable races of man, and Goldsby (1971), using basically the same criteria, lists 26. Garn (1971) in the third edition of *Human Races* stresses three levels of classification: geographical races, local races, and microraces. Table A4 lists some of the more important blood group differences for the three major racial groups. These three groups do not constitute definable breeding populations, but rather clusters of more or less related populations, living basically within the geographical bounds indicated in the table heading. Consequently, the listing of specific gene frequencies would be meaningless, in fact, not possible; thus, only relative incidences are given.

From the Linnaean system to present systems, using a variety of criteria, all classifications have consistently drawn lines at the major geographical boundaries. This can only be a consequence of the fact that these boundaries underlie the processes that are prerequisite to

Table A4. *Race and bloodgroups: relative incidence.*

System	Gene	Caucasoid (European)	Negroid (African)	Mongoloid (Asiatic)
ABO	A_2	Moderate	Moderate	Essentially absent
	B	Low	Intermediate	High
Rh	R^o	Low	High	Low
	r	High	Intermediate	Essentially absent
Duffy	Fy^a	Intermediate	Low	High
	Fy	Absent	High	Absent
Diego	Di^a	Absent	Absent	High
Sutter	Js^a	Absent	High	Absent

racial diversification. In the absence of a biological deterrent to fertile matings between members of two different populations, as occurs between species, geographical barriers or distance are the two most significant barriers to genetic exchange. The greatest distances and largest geographical barriers on earth are between the continents. Consequently, the genetic differences between the population centers of Europe, Asia, Africa, Australia, and the Americas are maximal for the human species. The geographically intermediate populations tend to be genetically intermediate as well. It was exactly this kind of problem with intermediate groups that confused all manner of earlier classification. While the classification of intermediate groups still has not been resolved, their existence is now better understood and sheds meaningful light upon the mechanisms of race formation and dissolution, and thereby upon the very mechanisms by which the evolution of a species takes place.

REFERENCES

Amadon, D. 1949. The seventy-five percent rule for subspecies. *Condor* 51: 250–258.

Boyd, W. C. 1950. *Genetics and the races of man.* Boston: Little, Brown.

Coon, C. S. 1965. *The living races of man.* New York: Knopf.

Dobzhansky, T. 1951. *Genetics and the origin of species.* New York: Columbia Univ. Press.

Dobzhansky, T. 1962. *Mankind evolving*. New Haven: Yale Univ. Press.

Garn, S. M. 1971. *Human races*, 3rd ed. Springfield, Ill.: Charles C Thomas.

Goldsby, R. A. 1971. *Race and races*. New York: Macmillan.

Hooton, E. A. 1947. *Up from the ape*. New York: Macmillan.

Simpson, George Gaylord. 1962. *Principles of animal taxonomy*. New York: Columbia Univ. Press.

Weiner, A. S. 1948. A classification of the ABO and Rh blood systems. *Amer. J. Phys. Anthrop.* 6: 236–237.

Glossary

Words are defined within the context of their use in the text. Words italicized within a definition are also defined in the Glossary.

Acetabulum The hip socket, or cup, into which the head of the femur or thigh bone fits.

Adaptation The process by which populations or organisms undergo changes that make them better able to survive and to reproduce in a given environment. The term may also be applied to an individual in terms of his ability to undergo anatomical, behavioral, developmental, and physiological changes that improve his ability to survive and reproduce.

Adolescence The period of life between puberty and adulthood during which sexual and physical growth is completed.

Allele An alternate form of a *gene* at a given position or *locus* on a *chromosome*. If two forms of a gene are designated *A* and *a*, then *A* is the allele of *a*, and vice versa. The blood groups A, B, O, and AB are determined by alleles.

Allopatric Occupying different geographic areas.

Anastomosis The joining of two or more tubular vessels. Usually used in relation to the cardiovascular system.

Antibody A specific and complex protein, which the body produces as a defensive response to a specific *antigen.*

Antigen A substance that is capable of stimulating the body to produce specific or neutralizing *antibodies.* It can be any foreign substance, such as pollen, tissue, or blood cells of a genetically different person, etc.

Arithmetic mean An average found by dividing the sum of a series of numbers by the number of items in the series.

Balanced polymorphism A *polymorphism* maintained in a population, usually as a result of the fact that the heterozygotes for the responsible *alleles* have a higher adaptive value than either of the *homozygotes.*

Behavioral genetics   The area of genetics that deals with the inheritance of different types or forms of behavior, such as intelligence, personality traits, and so forth.

Caucasoids   The name given to people of the so-called white race whose center of distribution is Europe.

Cell nucleus   The structure in most cells that contains the *chromosomes.*

Chromosomal aberration   An alteration in the normal number or structure of chromosomes. This may be a loss, a duplication, or a rearrangement of genetic material. Aberrations of particular chromosomes or of specific segments of a chromosome have a characteristic effect. *Down's syndrome* or mongolism is an example.

Chromosome   A deeply staining thread or body in the nuclei of cells that is composed primarily of nucleoproteins, especially *deoxyribonucleic acid,* which constitutes the molecular basis of heredity. Specific mutational sites along the chromosome are referred to as *gene loci.* In man, there are 23 pairs of chromosomes with a total of some thirty-thousand gene loci.

Class   See *Social class.*

Clines   A geographical gradient or gradual change in the frequency of a characteristic.

Consanguinity   A blood relationship between people because of the same ancestry or descent. The term is often used in descriptions of mating between relatives.

Contiguous populations   Two or more adjoining populations with varying degrees of contact and exchange.

Correlation coefficient   The degree to which statistical variables or measurements vary together. The coefficient has a value from zero to -1 or $+1$.

Deciduous teeth   The first or so-called "baby" teeth, which are replaced by the permanent dentition.

Deme   A local breeding population. The deme may be as large as a tribe or include a number of small communities.

Deoxyribonucleic acid   The critical component of the *chromosome* constituting the molecular basis of heredity.

Descent group   A lineage or group descending through many generations.

Diabetes   A disease characterized by defective sugar metabolism and excessive urination or polynuria.

DNA   See *Deoxyribonucleic acid.*

Down's syndrome (Mongolism)   Probably the most common developmental anomaly resulting from a *chromosomal aberration.*

Drift   See *Genetic drift.*

Dysautonomia (Riley-Day syndrome)   An autosomal recessive hereditary disease occurring mainly among Jews. Symptoms include: a decreased production of tears, a reduction in most sensory responses and reflexes, frequent seizures, and retarded skeletal growth.

Ecological   Referring to the physical environment of an organism.

Ectoderm   The germ layer from which the skin, hair, nails, brain, and nerve tissue are formed.

Embryonic development   Though often used to loosely define the total prenatal period of development, the term technically refers to the first trimester of prenatal growth.

Endemic diseases   Those diseases that are peculiar to a distinct area or class of people, and which have not been introduced from some outside source within recorded history.

Endogamy   Mating within a band, social group, or other defined breeding population. For example, in a situation of caste endogamy, mating is permitted only with members of the same caste.

Enzyme   A protein molecule that catalyzes a specific chemical reaction. Many enzyme variants in the red blood cells and serum are now known and can be demonstrated to be under simple genetic control.

Ethnic group   A group or population distinguished by common cultural characteristics.

Ethnocentrism   The feeling that one's own culture has a way of living, values, and patterns of adaptation superior to all others.

Etiology   The demonstrated cause of a trait or of a disease.

Evolution   The cumulative change in gene frequencies in the inherited characteristics of populations during the course of successive generations.

Gene   A hereditary unit at a fixed position or *locus* on a *chromosome* that has a specific effect on some characteristic and can change by *mutation*. The effect of a gene may be visible, e.g., eye color, or only detectible by special laboratory techniques, e.g., see *Hemoglobinopathies, Sicklemia*.

Gene flow   The spread of genes through distance, or across a traditional mating boundary as a consequence of mating with immigrants.

Gene frequency   The relative number of a particular form (*allele*) of a gene in a given population, expressed as a percentage.

Gene locus (plural: loci)   The position that a gene occupies on a chromosome.

Gene pool   The *genotype* of a population. The gene pool is the total of the genes possessed by the reproductive members of a definable population.

Genealogy   A family pedigree or lineage.

Genetic drift   Fluctuations in *gene frequencies* due to chance, the effects of which are most important in small populations, for example, under one hundred breeding individuals.

Genotype   The genetic constitution of an individual as distinguished from his physical or physiological properties (his *phenotype*).

Glucose-6-phosphate dehydrogenase deficiency   A genetically determined enzymatic abnormality, which results in a hemolytic anemia upon eating fava beans or being exposed to the drug primaquine.

Hardy-Weinberg law Both *gene frequencies* and *genotype* frequencies will remain constant from generation to generation in a breeding population in the absence of those forces that change gene frequencies: *selection, mutation,* migration, *genetic drift,* and *meiotic drive.* With a single pair of *alleles, A* and *a,* this is expressed as $p^2(AA): 2pq(Aa): q^2(aa)$. Where p is the dominant allele and q is the recessive allele.

Hemoglobins The oxygen-carrying pigment of red blood cells.

Hemoglobinopathies Genetically determined abnormalities of the *hemoglobins.*

Hemophilia A genetically determined disease characterized by defective blood clotting.

Heterosis (hybrid vigor) An increase in vigor, growth, survival, and fertility of *heterozygotes* relative to *homozygotes.*

Heterozygotes See *Heterozygous.*

Heterozygous The *alleles* at a given *locus* differ on the two members of a pair of *chromosomes,* e.g., $I^A I^B$ for blood group AB.

Homo sapiens In the classification of organisms into an evolutionary hierarchy, *Homo* is the name given to the genus in the family of primates containing man. *Sapiens* is the species designation within the *Homo* genus that includes all forms of modern man. *Erectus* is the name of the species that immediately preceded modern man. *Homo erectus* lived during the middle Pleistocene, between half a million and a million years ago.

Homozygotes See *Homozygous.*

Homozygous The *alleles* at a given *locus* are identical on the two members of a pair of *chromosomes,* e.g., $I^O I^O$ for blood group O.

Host factors The individual's defense mechanisms against infection and disease.

Hybridization The mating of genetically unlike individuals.

Inbreeding The mating of closely related individuals, those sharing one or more common ancestors.

Incest taboo The restrictions in all human societies against the mating of certain categories of relatives.

Indices A mathematically expressed relationship between two anatomical measurements.

Intrabreeding Mating only with individuals from the same population. Also termed *endogamy.*

Lability The capability of changing, perhaps in adapting to prevailing conditions of the environment.

Leukemia A disease of the blood in which there is persistent increase in leucocytes, or white blood cells, with changes in the spleen, bone marrow, or lymphoid system.

Lipoidoses Lipoids are fat-like substances, which occur in body cells and fluids. Lipoidoses are errors in the chemistry or metabolism of these substances.

Loci See *Gene locus*.

Mandible The lower jaw bone.

Maturation The achievement of full sexual and physical development.

Median The middle value in a group of numbers arranged in order of size. In referring to the median age of a group of individuals, one half of the individuals will be younger and one half will be older than the median age.

Meiotic drive The unequal recovery of the two types of ova or sperm produced by a heterozygote individual.

Melanin A dark pigment formed in the body and deposited in different amounts in the skin, hair, and nerve tissues.

Menarche The beginning of menstruation in human females during puberty.

Mendelian population A reproductive community among whom matings most frequently occur and who consequently share in a common *gene pool*.

Miscegenation Mating between members of different racial or *ethnic groups*.

Mode of inheritance The genetic determination of a *phenotypic* character is dependent upon the action of only one or two *gene loci* when we speak of a "simple" mode of inheritance.

Mongolism See *Down's syndrome*.

Mongoloids The name given to people of the so-called yellow race whose center of distribution is Asia. Sometimes it is extended to include the Indians of North and South America.

Monogenic character A qualitatively variable character under the control of *alleles* at a single *locus* in a *chromosome*, as, for example, sickling (see *Sicklemia*) and the ABO blood groups.

Morphology The visible physical structures of an organism; also the science dealing with the developmental and evolutionary history of these structures.

Muscular dystrophy A group of genetically determined diseases characterized by a progressive wasting of the musculature of the shoulders, hips, and limbs.

Mutation A heritable change in the *DNA* structure of a gene.

Nature-nurture problem The problems of determining the relative importance of the genetic and the environmental contribution to observed variation in a physical, physiological, or psychological trait or characteristic.

Negroids The name given to the so-called black race whose center of distribution and origin is Africa. It does not include the black-skinned people of India, the Pacific Islands, or Australia.

Orthoselection   The *selection* for those traits that most importantly benefit a group in adapting to their particular environment. An example is selection for learning ability in man, for whom the capacity to learn new and increasingly complex techniques has enhanced his ability to exploit his physical environment and thereby support even larger human populations.

Ossification   The closing of the growth centers of bone through bone formation or replacement of cartilage by bone.

Osteological data   Information derived from skeletal material.

Paresis   An incomplete state of paralysis.

Pentosuria   The chronic presence of pentose (one of the sugars) in the urine, occasionally mistaken for diabetes. This is a rare error in metabolism found most frequently among Jews.

Phenotype   The physical or physiological properties of an individual produced by the interaction of his *genotype* with his environment.

Phenylthiocarbamide   A chemical compound, often referred to as PTC, which is tasteless to some people but bitter to others. It occurs naturally in turnips, cabbage, and similar vegetables.

Phrenology   A cult or pseudo-science claiming to predict mental characteristics on the basis of the shape and conformation of the skull.

Phylogenetic   A relationship based upon evolutionary history.

Pleiotropy   A single *gene* is responsible for more than one *phenotypic* effect.

Polydactyly   More than five fingers or toes.

Polygenic character   A quantitatively variable character dependent upon the interaction of many genes at different *loci*, as for example stature, intelligence, etc. (see also *Monogenic character*).

Polymorphism   Two or more *alleles* at a given *locus* exist in a population. An example is that of the ABO blood group system.

Postnatal   Referring to the period of development after birth.

Primordial unicellular state   See *Zygote*.

Protohominids   Forms preceding, but believed to have given rise to, the family Hominidae, which includes all primates, including man.

Psychometric intelligence   Measured levels or facets of intelligence.

Puberty   The period at which the ability to reproduce is achieved. In the United States the age of puberty is legally defined as 14 for boys and 12 for girls.

Sarcoidosis   Multiple skin nodules or tumors.

Selection   Individuals with different *genotypes* will contribute different numbers of offspring to the next generation. Those leaving the largest number of offspring are then by definition the best adapted to that particular environment.

Septicaemia   Pathogenic bacteria in the blood.

Serology   The study of the production and interactions of *antibodies* and *antigens*.

Sickle-cell anemia   See *Sicklemia*.

Sicklemia (Sickle-cell anemia)   A severe disease affecting the red blood cells. At low oxygen tensions the cells become sickle- or crescent-shaped and are destroyed in large numbers. Individuals *homozygous* for this gene die at an early age. Individuals *heterozygous* for this gene are not severely affected and are more resistant to malaria.

Social class   A position within the total society usually designated as "low," "middle," or "high," based upon occupation, education, income level, housing, etc., which social scientists quantify to create a socioeconomic rating or index by which to judge individual families.

Sociolinguistics   A branch of sociology dealing with the interrelationship between the ability to communicate verbally and adjustment to social phenomena.

Species   A population or system of genetically related populations, all members of which are interfertile, but unable to mate with members of other species. This is the basic unit of evolution.

Spermatozoa   The mature male germ cell or gamete. Also called "sperm."

Subspecies   A geographic subdivision of a *species* based upon characteristics that distinguish it from other populations within the species. Also termed a "geographical race."

Sympatric   To coincide or overlap.

Taxonomic   A system of classification based upon evolutionary relationships.

Thalessemia (Cooley's anemia)   A genetically determined anemia. *Homozygotes* die in childhood. *Heterozygotes* have a milder form of the disease.

Zygote   The fertilized ovum resulting from union of the two gametes (ovum and sperm).

Index

Acclimatization to altitude and temperature, 27
Adaptability: human, defined, 8; race and culture in, 25-26; sources of human, 26-28. *See also* Adaptation
Adaptation: and evolution, 4, 31, 36-37; and culture, 22, 83-84; and human educability, 22, 27; breadth of human, 25-26; sources of human, 26-28; and stress, 27, 34-35; types of, 28, 33-35; and genetic variability, 28; population similarities in, 28; and population genotypes, 30; evidence for genetic, 31-33; psychological, 34, 35; population variation in, 35-36; of Eskimo, 69. *See also* Adaptability
Africans: skeletal maturation of, 42; tooth eruption of, 43, 44, 45; adult body proportions of, 51; gró́wth of Pygmies, 51; sickle cell among, 60; disease among, 72. *See also* Hutu, Tutsi
Albinism, 84
Altitude: effect on blood cells, 79-80; acclimatization to, 27; and delayed puberty, 46
Amadon's rule, 163
American Indians: tooth eruption of, 45-46; disease among, 63, 69; fossil remains of, 78; fertility of, 136
Anthropologists on race and intelligence, 115-116
Australopithecine, 80

Balanced polymorphisms, 71
Banneker group, 110-111
Biological distance explained, 4
Blood groups: race differences in, 17-18, 19; race classification by, 170, 171
Blumenbach, Johann Friedrich, 166

Caucasians: norms among, 70; origin of term, 166
Census of 1840, 87-88
Chinese: disease among, 63, 88, 89; fertility of, 136
Chromosomes: nature of, 14
Civil rights: racist response to, 20; and poverty, 125
Clines, 6
Cold, response to, 32
Culture: effect on human species, 13; and adaptation, 22, 25-26, 30, 83-84; effect on mating, 59, 60; as human universal, 80; and division of labor, 81; and language, 81, 82; and orthoselection, 83; and race differences, 84-85; of low-income groups, 128-132

Deoxyribonucleic acids, 14
Deprivation and intelligence, 100-101
Desegregation in schools, 111-113, 114
Disease: and selection, 57; and race, 60-66; major indices of, 60; among Jews, 60, 69, 71, 72; among Negroes, 61-63, 65, 72; among whites, 61-63, 72; among American Indians, 63, 69; among Chinese, 63, 88, 89; among Hawaiians, 63, 72; among Japanese, 63, 68; inherited disorders, 64, 66; by ethnic group, 66-67, 72; and evolution, 69; and environment, 71
Diversity: causes of human, 20; and equality of opportunity, 23

Educability: as adaptive trait, 22, 27; and human plasticity, 80
Education: for Negroes, 110-113; racial segregation in, 111-113, 114; and poverty, 125, 126; and minority groups, 126; and social class, 126-